What (

David Holland's book "I   /
spiritual experience. It i   ;
purity in their sexuality. '   into the bedroom
with God and invites him to express his pure desires to you
whether you are single or married.

Douglas Weiss, Ph.D.,
Author of "Clean: A proven plan for
men committed to sexual integrity"
Executive Director of Heart to Heart Counseling Center

David Holland has written a no nonsense, no holds barred
account of his personal deliverance from sexual addiction.
This content is not for the faint-hearted, and some may well
be offended or disturbed by its message. Jesus got the same
reaction to his preaching so David is in good company! A
sex-drenched culture that has lost its moral compass needs a
wake-up call, and this book could be it! Buy it, read it, share
it!

Pastor Doug Williams,
Senior leader of Emmanuel Christian Centre, London

David Holland has written about a topic that took much
courage and faith to produce; men's struggle with their sexual
urges. I doubt if there's any man on planet earth who hasn't
had some of his same struggles, IF they're honest. However
our God always leads us into triumph, if we will listen to
Him. David has made this an easily readable book which will
eliminate much guilt from the men who read it, and help
them to find their own personal victory in these and other
areas.

Rod Anderson, Founder of "The Prayer Foundation"
and Senior Leader of Commonwealth Church
Host of "Above it all", God TV

Dave has dared to bare-all with incredible honesty about his life and struggles in this fantastic book. 'Paying for Sex' is a must read for anyone tired of living an exhausting life of lies!

Melvyn Naidoo,
Senior Pastor at London City Life Church

Paying for Sex is a much needed book that will help to set people free. Dave's radical freedom from sexual addiction points to the power of Jesus! His book will help those who read it to love God and help others, producing mature, honest believers and disciples!

Gerald Coates,
Founder of the Pioneer movement of churches,
and author of "Sexual Healing"

PAYING FOR SEX

The Spiritual Implications
of Your Sex Life and Mine

DAVID HOLLAND

DUTCH HOUSE PUBLISHING

Copyright © 2013 by David Holland
ISBN: 978-0-9928109-0-0

Dutch House Publishing
www.DutchHousePublishing.com
dutchhousepublishing@gmail.com

DEDICATION

I dedicate this book to the countless Christians who find themselves entangled in a web of sexual addiction. I truly believe that what you are about to read has the power to launch you into a lifetime of lasting freedom.

Abbreviations of Bible Versions:

AMP	Amplified Bible
AKJV	American King James Version
ESV	English Standard Version
ESVUK	English Standard Version (United Kingdom Edition)
GWT	God's Word Translation
KJ2000	The King James 2000 Bible
KJB	King James Bible (Cambridge Edition)
KJV	King James Version
MSG	The Message: The Bible in Contemporary Language
NASB	New American Standard Bible
NIV	New International Version
NLT	New Living Translation
TNIV	Today's New International Version
WEY	Weymouth's New Testament in Modern Speech

Acknowledgments:

So many people played a significant part in this book coming together. Firstly I want to thank my parents who have been an amazing source of encouragement and support to me throughout this season of my life. My dad in particular has really helped me to make sense of the journey I have been on since February 2010.

For their editorial contributions to this book I want to thank Carolyn Curtis, Mark Stibbe and Bruce Garrison. Each of these great writers have helped to shape what you will read in this book.

I'd like to thank Lisa at Designs done now, for her tireless efforts putting together the cover of my book. I was really very happy with the final result.

I would like to acknowledge some great leaders, preachers and writers who have helped to influence my theology. Peter Horrobin, Jackie Pullinger-To, Neil T Anderson, Mark Driscoll, and John Bevere.

For believing in me and the message in this book I want to thank my dear friend Pastor Doug Williams. I also want to give my heartfelt thanks to Rod Anderson, and Douglas Weiss.

I want to give a special note of appreciation to my pastors Melvyn and Bex Naidoo; you guys are such quality friends. Serving and leading church with you continues to be a great experience.

Finally, I want to thank my great friend and flatmate of four years Bjorn Perera, whose life and example have taught me a lot about Jesus.

CONTENTS

CHAPTER 1

NIGHTS TO REMEMBER

It all began on a Wednesday night in February 2010.

In one sense it was a night like any other night; as I lay in my bed, my mind was filled with graphic sexual images. Events from the timeline of my sex life started to fill the screen of my heart, reminding me in forensic detail of the experiences I'd had and the rush these encounters had given. In no time at all an intense desire to masturbate overwhelmed me, followed immediately by a longing to satisfy my sexual appetite through the use of pornography.

I don't know about your nocturnal patterns, but there was nothing unusual in all of this for me. I'll be really honest with you: this kind of tussle was typical. It was a struggle that I had regularly fought and most often lost ever since I became sexually aware.

Only this time I won.

In the past I had fought the obsessive desire to masturbate by forcing myself to steer my thoughts away from sex. This battle could last anything from thirty minutes to an hour. Sometimes the struggle would end with me falling asleep exhausted. On other occasions I simply gave up and yielded to the temptation to relieve myself.

But this time I managed to subdue my urges and resist temptation and drift off to sleep.

And then, several hours later, it happened.

I woke up and encountered something that was to shake me to the very core of my being and change me unrecognisably. It was the most momentous experience of my life.

Heart Problems

Before I describe what happened, I want to tell you the story of the months leading up to it.

This all began in mid-November 2009.

One night I woke up with an unbearable pain in my chest. It was sharp and severe, as if a knife was being plunged in and out of my heart. It was accompanied by a tightening in my chest so crippling that at moments I could barely breathe. Eventually I was taken into hospital and given blood tests. I waited for several hours before the Accident and Emergency doctor came to speak to me. The shock on his face was evident. He told me that the blood tests were positive and that it appeared likely that I'd had a heart attack. The troponin levels (an enzyme signifying damage to the heart) were highly elevated and, to use his words, 'off the charts.'

I was immediately admitted to hospital and a process of poking and prodding me began. I stayed at Lewisham University Hospital for just under a month. The medical staff continued to monitor me and gave me an angiogram, a cardiac MRI, several echoes and a plethora of exploratory tests. I was eventually discharged with no conclusive diagnosis. I was told that, due to my age, it was extremely unlikely that I had had a heart attack, but they couldn't identify another cause for my symptoms.

On leaving the hospital, I went to my parent's place to recover. No sooner had I arrived than I immediately broke down in tears. The sobbing that ensued over the following four hours was uncontrollable. I had been through a major trauma and it had taken its toll emotionally. But I was not able to explain what had happened or why.

It was my mother, however, who provided a key.

'Dave, you're concerned about your heart condition,' she said, 'but God's concern is the condition of your heart!'

When she said that, the lights came on.

The health of my physical heart wasn't the real issue. It was my spiritual state that needed urgent attention.

From then on my parents and I decided to make this a focus of prayer. We agreed that while the hospital was at a loss as regards my diagnosis, God was not. We also agreed that while the hospital couldn't help me, God most certainly could. So we made a commitment to pray together for a minimum of fifteen minutes every day, without fail. And that is exactly what we did.

The results, though not immediate and not what I was expecting, were undeniably powerful.

Supernatural Encounters

And so we return to that momentous night in February 2010, just three months or so later.

I had somehow managed to triumph over my temptations that night. Then I fell asleep. Indeed, if there had been a camera positioned in my room, you would have seen me sleeping soundly from 11:30pm until 3:30am.

And then it happened.

Suddenly I found myself wide-awake and standing upright. I'd gone from a horizontal to a vertical position without even realising it and from sleep to consciousness in a matter of moments.

Arms flaying wildly in every direction, eyes wide open, face screwed up and contorted—I had no control over my physical body or my vocal chords.

I was confused, petrified and completely unsure of what was going on. I could hear myself screaming in a banshee-like tone, screeching out the name of Jesus. This must have lasted for about forty-five seconds. Such was its intensity that it actually bruised my vocal chords. Throughout it all, a sensation of what I can only describe as sheer evil was surging through my entire body. I was aware of it in my emotions but I was also conscious of it in my body. It was flooding outwards from the centre of my being even to my fingertips.

When this subsided, I saw directly in front of my eyes a misty and ghost-like substance.

I fell to the floor completely motionless.

After a few moments I realised that my entire body was dripping with sweat.

When I looked at my watch, the time was 3:32 a.m.

The next day I couldn't stop thinking about this episode. What had actually happened? What did it all mean?

Being a committed Christian, I picked up my New Testament and began to read again the many stories in the Gospels of Mark, Matthew and Luke in which Jesus set people free from unclean, evil spirits that had been tormenting them. Pretty quickly I realised what had happened. I had encountered the supernatural power of Jesus in my bedroom. He had set me free from an unholy spirit just as he did with others when he walked this earth two thousand years ago. This spirit had gone.

But I was not entirely free yet.

In fact, what happened next was more like something from a horror movie than the typical experience of a born-again Christian.

For three nights, almost as soon as I fell asleep, I would see a terrifying evil creature snarling at me. This would begin in a dream and it would cause me to sit up in my sleep, groaning in fear. Sometimes I would even see this creature as I came out of my sleep state into consciousness.

It seemed that whatever had been oppressing my soul was desperate to gain access again.

I decided to talk to my dad. I shared with him what had happened and that I was now living in continual fear. He asked if he could pray for me and I said yes.

My dad confronted any remnants of demonic oppression, telling every evil spirit to leave. As he prayed, I started to shake physically. My whole body quaked. This was no subtle, gentle shiver, but an aggressive, forceful tremor.

Clearly I was receiving more freedom.

Strong Deliverer

You won't be surprised to learn that I subsequently asked what all this meant.

In a short time of praying and studying the Scriptures, I came to the conclusion that Jesus Christ, the Strong Deliverer, had been setting me free from bondages which had had a strong hold over my life for many years.

In the first instance, Jesus had set me free from my bondage to compulsive lust.

The evidence for this was the context of this experience. The night before it happened I had been fighting the desire to indulge myself sexually. It was also confirmed by the fruit from it. Four years later, I am still living in complete freedom in this area of my life. From that day until now, I have had no issues with pornography or masturbation. In short, I have had no compulsive sexual urges. I now have complete control over my desires—something which would have been unthinkable in the previous eighteen years of my life.

My second encounter—which occurred when my dad prayed for me—involved being set free from three things which had also been afflicting me for years: fear, intimidation and depression. Since that encounter, I have lived completely free from their grip.

Prior to this, I had spent years being intimidated by dominant personalities. The fear of dealing with conflict would cripple me. I had also been struggling with depression—a problem which I had kept secret from everybody.

These three bondages had prevented me from functioning properly in my personal life, my ministry and my employment. Thank God these no longer hold me hostage. Freedom has come into my life and that freedom is more profound and real now than it was on the day it happened.

Paradigm Shifts

People talk about sudden changes in the way we think about life, the world, everything. These are often referred to as 'paradigm shifts'. That is exactly what happened to me.

Prior to that night in February 2010, I had no framework for such experiences. I knew that Jesus set people free from all sorts of oppression in his ministry two thousand years ago. But I didn't know that he still did this kind of thing today.

And I certainly didn't realise that he wanted to set believers free from sexual sin and its enslaving effects.

Here's what I came to see in my 'paradigm shift.'

First of all, there are what I call 'shadows' that afflict us when we sin sexually. Sex is not just a purely physical act. It is a profoundly spiritual experience. Although I'm single, I believe that in marriage this experience is meant to be beautiful, joyful and playful. It is something designed to bring a feeling of immense and intense spiritual unity and intimacy to a husband and wife. Outside of marriage, however, indulging one's flesh in acts of sexual immorality is equally spiritual—only this time it's unholy or unclean spirits that enter the picture. These shadows gain access to the souls of those who engage in sexual sin, whatever form that takes. As Peter Horrobin has written, 'it is rare to find that a person has not picked up demons through having immoral sexual relationships. Sex is primarily spiritual, and so when people enter into sexual relationships that are sinful, they should not be surprised that the demonic will take advantage of the channel that has been opened up through sin.'

At this point some of you may be asking, 'are you saying that a Christian can be controlled by demonic spirits if they sin sexually? Are you serious?'

In answering this, consider not only the wisdom of experienced Bible teachers but also my own testimony. At the time of my breakthrough, not every part of my body was under my control. Parts of my body were taken over by something external to me. I was aware of what was going on and indeed I was observing it. But I didn't personally initiate the events that played out. I didn't get out of bed of my own volition. I did not decide to start waving my hands about. I certainly wasn't responsible for the thunderous roar coming out of my lungs. At that moment what was happening to me felt much more than simply temptation or even oppression.

When it comes to spiritual darkness affecting Christians, we are far more comfortable with the language of temptation and oppression than weird words like 'possession.' I agree that this word isn't helpful because it implies ownership. Once a person becomes a Christian, Jesus is Lord of their lives, and they belong to him. That's a fact. However, while I am sure that Christians experience temptation and oppression regularly, I also have to give room to the idea that a Christian can experience more than these common forms of spiritual attack. Eventually, through repeated sexual sin, a Christian can become bound by a stronghold. At this point, the person affected by shadows is still in control but they have a very strong burden on them to behave in a particular way.

I know that this may be controversial but it is something that both the teaching of Scripture and my personal testimony confirm. By yielding constantly to the temptations of the flesh, a person isn't just doing something which affects them physically. They are opening a door in their souls and their spirits to shadows—to unclean spirits. When that happens, the darkness afflicting them can no longer be said to be external. It has become internal as well.

This is something new that I have had to acknowledge.

Okay, that's the bad news.

Now here's the good news.

The second truth I have come to acknowledge is that Jesus is passionate about liberating us from everything that oppresses us, and at every level of our lives—the physical, emotional, and spiritual levels. Jesus offers us 'holistic freedom'—freedom in our spirits, souls and bodies.

He also offers us 'complete freedom', not just partial freedom. 'He whom the Son sets free is free indeed!' Jesus Christ can set us free from the most powerful of strongholds and the most malicious of shadows. This is why freedom ministry must not be overlooked when it comes to sexual addictions.

This book is accordingly an exploration of these two big ideas—that sexual acts have spiritual implications and that Jesus can set us free from those 'shadows' that start to torment us when we became slaves to sexual immorality.

It is a message that's come out of my mess.

Now I appreciate that this is not just raw in its honesty but also radical in its emphasis and in that respect some of you may already think I've lost the plot. Indeed, you may even be laughing at all this or in the process of chucking my book in your bin.

My advice is to consider not just my testimony but also, much more importantly, my teaching from the Bible.

If you give me a fair hearing, you may find that Jesus Christ brings you a level of insight and freedom you never thought possible.

Yes, there is a destructive payback for sexual sin, which is why this book is called *Paying for Sex.*

But it's equally true that nothing is too difficult or too dark for Jesus to deal with it, and decisively.

He is the same yesterday, today and forever (Hebrews 13.8).

He hasn't ever stopped being our Strong Deliverer.

Any thoughts on this chapter? Participate in the conversation on twitter: @pfsbook #nightstoremember or www.facebook.com/pfsbook

CHAPTER 2

LIKE A VIRGIN

I am a virgin. I'm in my thirties, and I have not yet had sex. I'm waiting for marriage before I get around to losing my virginity. There are actually a lot of us out there. Maybe you are one of us. Some of you may despair at the fact that I have not been there yet. Others may be saluting my resolve.

Before those of you who don't fit the 'virgin' category start to commend me, pause and consider the following question: if someone has pushed every boundary they can without actually having sexual intercourse, do they really fit the definition of 'virgin'? Or is it just a technicality?

Hanging onto virginity by a thread is not sexual purity.

Some people I know genuinely believe that they are virgins because they have not had sex. The problem is that they believe sex means only one thing. Sex is not sex unless the penis actually enters the vagina—unless there is actual penetration. This very narrow understanding means that many of us are welcome to 'the virgin club'.

Unfortunately, our membership has just expired!

We may be 'like a virgin', but we are not virgins.

I remember a conversation I had with a good friend of mine. He was defending his position following a decision to sin sexually. He brought an interesting argument to the table.

He was highlighting the fact that simple human physiological mechanics mean that a man and a woman are designed to connect sexually. He was quite convincing. How can we argue with the mechanics of nature? Our bodies were designed by God. Ergo, God must be fine about us using them in this way.

'I'm not being funny, Dave, but my bits were created with the specific purpose of going into her bits. I am physiologically drawn into this. It can't be that sinful if my body was designed for this!'

It's natural, right?

But is it truly in line with what God wants for us?

I recall another conversation I had with a friend from my church youth group. I must have been about fifteen at the time. The conversation turned to girls (as it often did) and specifically to what were the acceptable sexual boundaries in relationships for Christian young people like us. I was a few years younger than my friend and quite impressionable. He made it clear that he felt that anything other than penetrative sex was absolutely fine for Christians as it didn't technically qualify as sex. At the time this didn't quite sit right with me but gradually, through repeated conversations with this friend and others who shared his beliefs, I began to think that my own conservative approach needed to be loosened. Surely it wouldn't be unreasonable for me to adjust my boundaries a little.

Using a convenient technicality, my friends in these stories had persuaded themselves that they were virgins and therefore pure in God's eyes.

Why couldn't I follow suit?

Eventually, my convictions inevitably became diluted.

I embraced the 'like a virgin' view and settled for a compromised lifestyle. I began to look for holes in my beliefs in order to justify my unholy behaviour.

There's Something about Mary

There are many Christians today who believe that behaving like a virgin is the same as being a virgin. In other words, engaging in sexual acts which fall short of penetration is the same as refraining altogether from sexual acts and living a life of joyful abstinence.

Those who think this way should take a good look at the original Madonna, the Mother of Jesus.

Originally called *Miriam*, Mary was a young Jewish woman—possibly what we would call a teenager—when she was told by an angel that she would conceive a child by the Holy Spirit. This is exactly what happened and Joseph, her betrothed, came to understand this as a result of a dream.

This astounding miracle is known by Christians as the 'immaculate conception'—immaculate because the young Miriam had never had sexual relations of any kind in her life before and was totally chaste and pure. The innocent Miriam was to conceive a child supernaturally.

Let's develop this further. In terms of her sexual expression, Mary was a virgin. She had not had sexual intercourse, nor had she engaged in sexual acts. She had been living a life of chastity, remaining available to God in preparation for serving him. She was not 'like a virgin', she *was* a virgin. Unlike the present day Madonna, the first Madonna stood for sexual holiness.

Please think for a moment about the character and especially the integrity of this woman Mary. Was Mary, the mother of Jesus, just a 'technical' virgin? Had she been sexually active in Nazareth in every possible way, other than penetrative sex, with Joseph, or with other men, before the angel arrived to announce her pregnancy? If she had, would we still be comfortable calling her 'the Virgin Mary'? It is ludicrous to even suggest this. Mary was pure and living a life of authentic holiness. And the same should be true of us as we invest in our relationship with Jesus.

Let me be quite clear. Mary's sex life had implications too—positive ones. Mary's 'submitted' sexuality and purity meant she was ready to move as she was led by him. The result was that she was close enough to God to be chosen to be involved in the greatest plan in history as the mother of the coming Messiah, the saviour of the world, Jesus Christ. Mary was therefore not hanging onto her virginity by a thread. She was a consecrated woman with a heart after God. Sexual purity was self-evidently a priority for her.

Sex is Spiritual

As a result of my experiences described in chapter one, I became particularly alert to the spiritual nature of sex and the importance of not buckling to the pressures of temptation when they hit. I just knew that there was a spiritual dimension to what I was dealing with. I imagine that when Mary was visited by an angel and became aware of God's plan for her life, the very idea of 'doing stuff' with her fiancé Joseph and sinning sexually before marriage was far from her mind. That would mean contaminating what God was doing in her and her future during her pregnancy. Why would she do that?

How can we imitate Mary in terms of sexuality? One way is that we choose to remain pure till marriage, even during engagement. One reason for doing this is that we do not want to trade our intimacy with God for a corrupt premature experience of intimacy with someone to whom we are not yet married. Even if we 'love' someone, if we're not married, any sexual act can open up a door that will damage us spiritually. Fooling around is folly.

'Fooling around' refers to casual sexual activity, to sexual acts that don't involve intercourse. Many of my fellow-Brits believe that this expression originates from our American cousins with their slightly more laid back approach to life. 'Fooling around', suggests a more diluted and blasé attitude towards what happens between people who are feeling 'in the mood.' We're just fooling around. It's just a bit of fun; it doesn't mean anything.

This idea of 'casual sex' is seemingly irresistible in popular culture. It is perpetuated by TV, movies and many of the people with whom we live and work. It permeates everyday chitchat and it's regarded as a perfectly acceptable topic for anecdotal conversation. 'So what did you get up to at the weekend?'

It seems that, as a society, we have succumbed to and embraced this as an ethic. For those who choose to see sex as nothing but a bodily function, the irony of the term 'casual sex' appears to have been lost. This idea is of course an elephant of an oxymoron. Sex is not and should never be labelled as casual.

Sex is serious and sex is spiritual.

Some people genuinely believe they can detach themselves from the emotional and spiritual aspects of sex. They have convinced themselves that it can be enjoyed purely as an animalistic exercise and that it has no further implications. It seems that they are tragically unaware of the spiritual implications of sex. Most tragic of all is the fact that this ignorance has not only taken root in society; it has also become embedded in church culture, as is evident in the social and indeed sexual interactions between Christians. While some Christians would take a firm stance on sexual purity, and have boundaries and restrictions in place, many—including me—have at some point diluted our once steely convictions to accommodate a life of compromise.

But what has the cost been?

Joyful Abstinence

Some of you might be asking at this point how it's possible to be self-controlled and holy in such a sexualised culture. How is that achievable?

I want to be clear right from the start here. True sexual purity and abstinence is not achieved by the keeping of rules but by the grace of God. Self-control is, after all, a fruit of the Spirit so we can't do without God's help if we are to exercise restraint. Self-control grows in us as we nurture our relationship with God and develop intimacy with him. For those of us who are unmarried, and therefore have no righteous outlet for sexual expression, abstinence and sexual purity will appear in our lives as we nurture intimacy with God. For those of you who are married, and yet struggle with adultery, pornography or sexual impurity of any kind, the same truth applies.

The Singaporean preacher, Joseph Prince, has made a big impact on me through his teaching on the grace of God. One of his best quotes is particularly helpful when thinking about 'self-discipline'. He says, 'if I by my own self-discipline broke away from the power of sin, I would need my own self-discipline to keep me there! If by God's power I am set free in a particular area, it is he who will keep me in it'.

What Prince is saying is that we cannot attain let alone maintain a self-disciplined life without the empowering presence of God helping us. In short, we need God's power in addition to our will power.

Before my breakthrough moment, I spent a long time pursuing sexual purity. During that time I honestly didn't 'get it'. I didn't understand the value of holiness. A deep-seated regret over 'missing out' lurked just inches beneath the surface of my thoughts. I would hear of the sexual exploits of friends and colleagues and, though not actually saying it out loud, I would reflect on my own prudish existence and despair at the lack of notches on my bedpost.

Since February 2010, I have had a completely different view. The joy of abstinence has trumped the pleasures of 'casual sex.' My new life has been one of self-discipline. I have not masturbated. I have not had sex and I have not had an orgasm. With God's empowering grace, I have managed to conquer temptation.

In addition I have been given the grace to speak about this to others, even to those who find it difficult to embrace and understand and who argue that abstinence is dangerous on a physical and psychological level—and that we need to be sexually active to stay balanced and healthy.

But is this really the case? Let me ask you a vital question.

What has potential to affect us more: not expressing our sexuality to the alleged detriment of our flesh or actively expressing it to the actual detriment of our spirit?

You think that by restricting yourself to everything less than penetrative sex you are protecting yourself and therefore not opening the door to the enemy. Maybe you think that because you are using contraceptives you are 'safe'. But have you considered that sexual acts which fall short of intercourse might open the door to your soul? What about your private, habitual behavioural patterns? What makes you think that you are not drinking from a poisoned spiritual chalice when you engage in non-penetrative or private sexual acts?

Our lives are often compared to a house. If you invited all the wrong kinds of people over to a house party (among the guest list are arsonists, burglars and convicts), you cannot expect your house to be unaffected by that. Eventually, guests like these will damage, rob or destroy the place.

If you leave all the windows and doors of your house open, you should not be surprised if burglars enter and help themselves to your belongings. It will happen; it is just a matter of time.

So it is with the house of our lives.

We should understand that engaging in sexual acts outside of the marriage context is like inviting unwanted, destructive guests into our souls.

These dark guests I call 'shadows.'

The Bible calls them 'unclean spirits.'

Similarly, failing to exercise self-restraint and put up proper boundaries will eventually lead to you being robbed not just spiritually but also in the area of your sexuality.

With God's power and your will power, you can live a different life.

You don't have to live 'like a virgin.'

You can actually be a virgin.

You can live a life of joyful abstinence.

Any thoughts on this chapter? Participate in the conversation on twitter: @pfsbook #likeavirgin or www.facebook.com/pfsbook

CHAPTER 3

EXAGGERATING *EROS*?

In 1995 a twenty two year old woman called Monica Lewinsky began working at the White House as an intern for US President Bill Clinton. She subsequently entered into a relationship with the married President. Not long afterwards, Lewinsky confided in her friend Linda Tripp that she was having an affair and shared some of the details. Unknown to her, Tripp recorded the conversation and passed the tapes on to Kenneth Starr, who was already investigating Clinton on other matters.

News of the scandal broke out and on the 26th January 1996 Clinton appeared with his wife Hilary at a White House press conference. In a prepared statement he made what arguably became the most famous sound bite of his presidency. 'I did not have sexual relations with that woman.'

Later, it transpired that what Clinton meant was that he had not had intercourse with Lewinsky. But they had done pretty well everything short of that. In the end, it was the revelation of a semen-stained blue dress that gave the game away. In a grand jury testimony in July of the same year, Clinton admitted that he had had an 'improper physical relationship.'

Distorting Reality

I begin with this story not only because it highlights what I was saying in the last chapter—that people conveniently redefine what is meant by 'sexual relations'—but also because it shows how we can distort reality to suit our own purposes. Clinton distorted his view of what sex is when he denied the charge that he had had an affair. We shouldn't be judgmental about this. We can do this too.

Distorting reality is something that I believe happens when people say that sex isn't sex unless it involves penetration—that you are still a virgin if you've done everything but have intercourse.

But some of you may also be thinking that I'm guilty of distorting reality as well. You may be saying to yourself, 'he's guilty of exaggeration when he says that there are spiritual implications to sex.'

I don't deny that this might seem a compelling point to those who hold it. After all, we all tend to distort reality when it's convenient. Put another way, we are all prone to changing our beliefs if it justifies our behaviour.

Let me ask you, have you ever distorted reality in order to get what you want? I know I have. It is amazing how we can conveniently move the proverbial goal posts to create an alibi for our actions, especially in the context of sex. If you have blood flowing through your veins, you too will at some point have made measured decisions to follow a path of compromise in your sex life.

But am I now guilty of the exact reverse? Am I creating a belief system to justify my celebration of abstinence? Am I distorting reality when I say that there are spiritual implications to our sexual acts? Am I guilty of over-thinking and exaggerating *eros*—by which I mean 'the expression of the sexual, the erotic, in human relationships'?

Maybe I am.

Maybe I should just be 'getting on with it' and setting my internal GPS to destination Pleasureville.

No Exaggeration

Even a cursory reading of the Bible will show you that from God's perspective physical acts have spiritual ramifications, that what we do with our bodies has implications when it comes to our spiritual life.

Let's consider two passages very briefly. The first will show us the positive spiritual implications of physical behaviour, the second the negative.

We begin with the positive. In a verse familiar to most Christians, the Apostle Paul teaches his readers about the kind of worship in which God delights: 'Therefore, I urge you, brothers, in view of God's mercy, to offer your bodies as living sacrifices, holy and pleasing to God—this is your spiritual act of worship' (Romans 12:1). Paul here 'urges', and in the King James Version 'beseeches', his readers to offer their bodies as living sacrifices. Paul is obviously keen to stress the importance of his teaching.

What is he saying then? Paul is proposing that there is a connection between physical behaviour and spiritual consequences. In this particular context he is stating that the offering of our physical bodies in obedient living is a spiritual act of worship. He is saying that our physical behaviour, when submitted to God's ways, has good spiritual implications. It results in holiness—in other words, a life of wholeness as God defines it. It also attracts the pleasure of God. It pleases him. Submitting our bodies to righteous living is therefore spiritually enriching. It has immensely positive, life-giving and healthy consequences.

Here is our second passage:

'You can't say that our bodies were made for sexual immorality. They were made for the Lord and the Lord cares about our bodies... Don't you realize that our bodies are actually parts of Christ? Should a man take his body, which is part of Christ, and join it to a prostitute? Never! And don't you realize that if a man joins himself to a prostitute, he becomes one with her? For the Scriptures say, "The two are united into one." But the person who is joined to the Lord is one spirit with him.' Run from sexual sin! No other sin so clearly affects the body as this one does.' (1 Corinthians 6:13-17, NLT).

Here Paul explores the other side of the same coin he's been looking at in Romans 12. If the godly use of our bodies produces positive spiritual results, the ungodly use of our bodies has the opposite effect. If worshipping God in a bodily way releases spiritual life and health to us, worshipping sex in a bodily way has the exact opposite effect. What we do with our bodies therefore has spiritual implications. This is especially true in the case of sexual sin which is why Paul says run away as far as you possibly can from sexual immorality. 'No other sin so clearly affects the body as this one does.'

But you may say, 'Paul only says that sexual sin affects the body here, so how can you claim that he says that it opens a door to spiritual darkness?'

I say it because Paul clearly teaches that sex is a life-uniting act in which two become one—and not just one physically, but spiritually too.

If you have sex with a prostitute (Paul's specific subject in the Corinthian situation), you unite with that person at a spiritual not just a physical level.

And if you unite with God through a physical act of worship, your spirit unites to his Spirit. 'The person who is joined to the Lord is one spirit with him.'

When you unite with another person outside of marriage through sexual acts, your spirit unites to their spirit. This offering of your body to someone else—instead of to God—becomes your spiritual act of worship. You are worshipping that person with your body.

Consequently, a door is opened to more than just physical thrills. It is opened to shadows.

That's no exaggeration.

Extreme Christianity

Is Paul distorting reality and being over the top when he suggests that the act of offering our bodies in sexual acts has spiritual implications too?

It may be that we do not fully grasp the significance of these spiritual implications, particularly in the context of sexual sin. While we are 'in the moment', we have more pressing things on our minds. In a room with a member of the opposite sex—kissing, touching and indulging in acts of sexual intimacy—for some inexplicable reason our priorities change.

Speaking for myself, whenever I found myself with a beautiful woman in this kind of compromising situation, I was thinking about the fulfilment of my physical and emotional needs, and hers too. Any other implications were far from my mind, especially spiritual ones. In rare moments when such scruples did surface, I buried them in a hidden place where fulfilment would not be interrupted by conscience.

While I was crossing boundaries with a girlfriend, kissing somebody I barely knew at a party, or masturbating while watching pornography, nobody told me that I could be in danger of inviting shadows into my life. I knew it wasn't pleasing God, but come on, opening doors to demonic realities?

If you'd said that to me before my breakthrough I would have probably replied that this all sounds like the stuff of myth or ghost story. You may be thinking that right now. But believe me—we're not talking about the Easter bunny or the tooth fairy here!

This is very real.

As you filter your previous and present behaviour through the colander of what I'm sharing in this book, can you remain as convinced as you once were that your sexual acts don't have spiritual consequences? Are you prepared to dismiss in a cavalier fashion the teaching of Scripture and the ramifications of my testimony?

All I can say is that what the Bible teaches and what I myself have experienced is not a case of exaggerating *eros* or distorting reality. It is the exact opposite. Indeed, my story should serve as a constant reminder of the dangers of denial in this area.

The Greatest Example

It may be that you still need convincing from the Bible that what we do with our bodies has spiritual implications. If so, consider the most important example of all. I'm talking about Jesus.

It's time we talked about him.

If ever someone's life and death proved the link between physical acts and spiritual implications, it was Jesus'.

Consider first of all his life.

The Christian faith rests upon the truth that when Jesus Christ was born, the infinite became an infant. God who is Spirit became a physical, human being.

This is known as the Incarnation, meaning that God took on flesh, that Jesus Christ is God with skin on.

In the Incarnation, God reveals for all time the connection between the physical and the spiritual.

Consider secondly his death.

The Christian faith also rests on the truth that when Jesus died physically he accomplished something which had momentous spiritual implications. Jesus came to earth to live a sinless life in a physical body so that on the Cross he could take the sin of the world upon his shoulders. In doing this, Christ through his physical death created a spiritual bridge between imperfect people and a perfect God. Through his physical sufferings and death, Jesus Christ acted as the sinless mediator between man and God. He paid the price. He bridged the gap. As a result, we who were all in the wrong in God's sight are now in the right. This is purely because Jesus Christ lived a totally righteous life in his body. Therefore, at Calvary, we who are unrighteous receive Christ's righteousness, provided that we repent of our sins and put our trust in him.

Who then can possibly argue that when Christ offered his body as a living sacrifice that it did not have mighty spiritual implications?

Listen again to the Apostle Paul as he celebrates just some of the spiritual results of Christ's physical death: 'having cancelled the charge of our legal indebtedness, which stood against us and condemned us; he has taken it away, nailing it to the cross. And having disarmed the powers and authorities, he made a public spectacle of them, triumphing over them by the cross' (Colossians 2:14, 15 TNIV).

At the Cross, Jesus was stripped naked, humiliated and physically nailed to a cross. He was forced to endure horrendous torture before being brutally put to death. This process was a very real physical experience. But the reality is that it was not solely limited to the bodily or physical realm. His death on the cross had an extraordinarily powerful spiritual effect too. Though it was not visible to the naked eye, something was going on spiritually during Jesus' crucifixion. What was it? The above verse in Colossians describes it to us. It says that when Jesus was crucified he disarmed and put to shame the powers of darkness and triumphed over them. His physical obedience led to spiritual victory over the devil and his army of shadows. His physical obedience resulted in their downfall.

In light of this, we must take measures not to cause a great divorce between physical actions and spiritual consequences. This may be how the world looks at reality, but it certainly isn't how the Bible looks at it. In the Biblical worldview, bodily acts and spiritual consequences are not separable. In the Bible, there is no division between what our culture today calls the secular and the sacred.

What we do with our bodies matters. Indeed, our bodies are meant to be temples of the Holy Spirit.

No More Snobbery

You may be saying, 'that's all very well, but the idea that there are negative spiritual implications to physical things, particularly something as natural and functional as sex, is untrue. You believe that misplaced sexual relationships can result in a 'demonic' problem? What a primitive notion!' I can hear you now, 'why is this guy still harping on about spiritual implications and shadows?'

For us to humble our minds and take on board things that don't make sense naturally can be very difficult. When we read the Bible, we have to respond to it with a spiritual rather than a natural mind—with the help of the Holy Spirit rather than simply with our human faculty of reason. We have to make a choice between believing the perfect revelation of the Bible or the imperfect reasoning of our culture.

When sophisticated people hear apparently 'extreme' Christians suggesting that emotional or physical problems might have a spiritual or demonic cause, many of them snigger and shake their heads in disbelief. As far as they are concerned, modern science is ample proof that there are other rational and sensible explanations for these things.

Please don't misread me here—your education and success are admirable. In many cases God supports your intellectual achievements. At the same time, please remember that God's message is designed to be accessible. Indeed, sometimes Biblical truth is easier to understand if you come at it with the innocence and trust of a child. Too much analysis can interfere with the clear message that God wants to convey. Too much reasoning rooted in earthly culture can dilute and distort the revelation which comes from the culture of heaven.

Listen to what happens in Luke 10.17-21 when Jesus commends the disciples who have gone in pairs on a mission to preach about the Kingdom of God and to heal the sick:

'The seventy-two returned with joy and said, "Lord, even the demons submit to us in your name."

He replied, "I saw Satan fall like lightning from heaven. I have given you authority to trample on snakes and scorpions and to overcome all the power of the enemy; nothing will harm you. However, do not rejoice that the spirits submit to you, but rejoice that your names are written in heaven."

At that time Jesus, full of joy through the Holy Spirit, said, "I praise you, Father, Lord of heaven and earth, because you have hidden these things from the wise and learned, and revealed them to little children. Yes, Father, for this is what you were pleased to do"' (Luke 10:17-21).

Verse 21 states that 'these things' (things concerning the Christian's authority over evil spirits) have been hidden from the 'wise and learned'. Clever and intelligent people apparently have trouble accepting the reality of demons and the devil. Their sophisticated reasoning acts as an obstacle to simple but life changing revelation.

It was C. S. Lewis who coined the brilliant phrase 'chronological snobbery'. His argument was that the thinking of an earlier time can seem *inherently* inferior when compared to that of the present. We can feel superior in understanding compared to previous generations. Simply put, we know better! We are on a far higher intellectual plane. We are highly evolved, superior in education and not about to be caught up in primitive, mythological beliefs.

Satan and demons!

Spiritual implications!

Perrlease!

To those who think this way, I would simply want to point to the words of Jesus in the passage above where it says about these truths that God has '...revealed them to little children'. The wise and the learned are not in the loop. The little children 'get it'. Get what? They understand that the devil is real, demons are real, but that as Christians we have spiritual authority to triumph over the forces of darkness.

As you travel with me through this book, try not to let the apparently sophisticated ideas of today's culture lead you into looking down with 'chronological snobbery' on Biblical teaching about sexual, physical acts.

Sit under Scripture. Don't stand over it.

Listen to God's Word with childlike faith. Don't judge it with intellectual arrogance.

Invite the Holy Spirit into your thinking.

God does not exaggerate when he talks about the spiritual implications of extra-marital *eros*.

His Word doesn't distort reality.

It defines it.

Any thoughts on this chapter? Participate in the conversation on 🐦 twitter: @pfsbook #exaggeratingeros or 📘 www.facebook.com/pfsbook

CHAPTER 4

THE SLIPPERY SLOPE

By now you may be asking, is it really possible for unclean spirits to afflict me as a Christian? All this talk of shadows, do they really exist? And if they do, how come they can get such a strong hold over my thoughts, feelings and choices, especially in the area of my sexuality?

If you're asking these sorts questions, that means not only that you've continued reading this far (well done for that!) but that you are thinking deeply about your own freedom or the freedom of a loved one.

So let's cut to the chase and deal with the questions.

The most important truth I want to get across in this chapter is that Christians can indeed become afflicted by evil spirits when they engage in sexual sin. In my case, eighteen years of habitual masturbation and pornography opened a door of my life to destructive demonic forces. In other words, part of my life—my sexuality—was under the control of unclean spirits. I refused to submit my sexuality to God's rule and in the process submitted it to self-rule (which the Bible calls 'sin'). As a result, over the course of time my sexuality became submitted to demonic rule.

Part of the evidence for the high level of control over my sexuality was what happened when I started to receive my freedom. My first experience of this was dramatic. I woke up in the middle of the night and found myself screaming, and then shaking violently. This is exactly what we see in the Gospels of Matthew, Mark and Luke when Jesus delivers people from demons. Look at what happens in the very first miracle that Jesus performs in Mark's Gospel, in the synagogue at Capernaum:

> *And immediately there was in their synagogue a man with an unclean spirit. And he cried out, "What have you to do with us, Jesus of Nazareth? Have you come to destroy us? I know who you are—the Holy One of God."*

> *But Jesus rebuked him, saying, "Be silent, and come out of him!" And the unclean spirit, convulsing him and crying out with a loud voice, came out of him.*

(Mark 1:23-26, English Standard Version)

This is a dramatic encounter!

Notice that the man was under the control of these demonic entities. It is his voice but their words that Jesus hears.

Notice also that there is more than one of these shadows. When the voice speaks, it speaks of 'us' not 'me'.

Notice finally that the man shakes violently (as in a convulsion) when Jesus sets him free.

That's hardly surprising. These shadows had exerted a very strong hold over the man. They didn't want to go without a struggle. But they were no match for the almighty and superior power of Jesus. They never are. So Jesus shook the man free from his bondage. His chains fell off. He was free.

Now the Scriptures do not record what the man did to invite these demons into his life. In a sense that is unimportant here. What is important is for us to understand that being in a synagogue or a church, or a member of a synagogue or a church, does not immunise us against spiritual oppression, and that only Jesus can set us free if our life comes under the control of shadows. He has supreme authority. 'Even evil spirits obey his orders!' (Mark 1.27).

So let's get one thing straight. Evil spirits do exist. They want to gain access to our lives as Christians because they want to immobilise us and render us ineffective as God's adopted sons and daughters.

This is not primitive, unsophisticated thinking. Jesus believed that these shadows existed and dealt with them. If he did, then we should.

The Cycle of Addiction

How is it possible, then, for such shadows to neutralise me as a Christian?

The answer is that this happens over time—that there is a process which leads to this level of demonic control.

If you look at the Book of James in the New Testament, you'll find a very revealing passage about this.

'Each person is tempted when they are dragged away by their own evil desire and enticed. Then, after desire has conceived, it gives birth to sin; and sin, when it is full-grown, gives birth to death.'

(James 1:14-15)

There are at least three stages mentioned here.

There is first of all the stage of desire. A Christian begins to experience a craving for something which the Bible forbids. Let's say it's lusting after images of sexual acts on the internet.

This then leads to a second stage which is called 'sin.' In other words, the desire—if not checked—leads to deeds, to watching pornography.

This eventually leads to a third stage, death—a total takeover of that person's life by increasingly extreme forms of pornography, leading to depression and ultimately even to death—including the death of one's relationships.

What the Apostle James has given us here is a very helpful—albeit disturbing—cycle of addiction.

The three stages can be described by the words 'enticement,' 'enactment', and 'entrapment.'

You can see these in the diagram below.

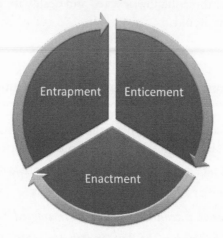

In the **enticement** stage, some form of addictive behaviour starts to appear attractive, appealing and alluring to a person. In spite of all reasonable arguments from Scripture, that person begins to yield to the deception that it's okay to submit to this unhealthy behaviour, relationship or substance.

This then progresses to the **enactment** stage—acting out the desire in behaviour patterns which, over the course of time, not only become habitual but compulsive.

This then leads inevitably to a third stage which is **entrapment**. The person becomes a slave to the behaviour, relationship or substance and is so powerless under its control that their lives effectively end and they become a pale reflection of their former selves. In this final stage they have ceased to be submitted to God and are submitted instead to their addiction, to their idol.

This third stage is the stage of complete bondage. It is the stage at which the addiction as opposed to God has become the person's master. To use the technical word, in this stage we are now under the sway of a demonic 'stronghold' (2 Corinthians 10.4).

A stronghold, as Ed Silvoso explains is 'a mindset impregnated with hopelessness that causes us to accept as unchangeable situations we know are contrary to the will of God.' It is a mindset which leads to not only despair but depression and not only depression but death.

Believe me when I say bondages are demonic, dangerous and destructive.

It's not just my testimony that teaches this.

More importantly, it is the infinite wisdom and the absolute truth of Scripture.

The Magdalene Story

At the beginning of Luke chapter 8 we are introduced to one of the most beautiful and memorable characters in the Gospels, Mary Magdalene.

'After this, Jesus travelled about from one town and village to another, proclaiming the good news of the kingdom of God. The Twelve were with him, and also some women who had been cured of evil spirits and diseases. Mary (called Magdalene) from whom seven demons had come out; Joanna, the wife of Chuza, the manager of Herod's household; Susanna; and many others. These women were helping to support them out of their own means' (Luke 8:1-3, NIV).

Notice that Luke chapter 8 begins with the words, 'after this.'

After what?

The answer is 'after what happened at the end of Luke chapter 7.' There we read about a Pharisee called Simon who invited Jesus to dinner at his home. During the meal, a woman who had been leading an immoral life entered the room and started wiping Jesus' feet with her tears, then kissing them, before finally pouring perfume on them. She was clearly in a place of repentance and was desperate for forgiveness and freedom.

Simon the Pharisee is enraged. 'If Jesus knew what kind of woman this is, what kinds of things she has done, he'd never let her do this.'

But Jesus reads Simon's heart and tells him that the person who is forgiven much, loves much. The person who has been forgiven little, loves little.

He then turns to the woman and says, 'your sins are forgiven. Your faith has saved you. Go in peace' (Luke 7.36-50 NIV).

Many Bible scholars believe that the woman in this story is none other than Mary Magdalene. It is directly 'after this' incident that reference is made to the women who followed Jesus. They did so out of great gratitude because Jesus had set them free from demons and disease. Mary Magdalene is especially singled out in this regard. Luke—who we should remember was a physician and fascinated by illness and its cure—tells us specifically that seven demons came out of her. This must surely be the same person who interrupted Simon the Pharisee's dinner party. She had clearly lived an immoral life and it seems that this had caused her to become oppressed by shadows.

Here then we see a hint of that connection I'm convinced exists between sexual immorality and unclean spirits.

If we wilfully yield control of our lives to any kind of sexual sin, we should not be surprised if we end up with shadows and then strongholds.

Mary Magdalene encountered the kindness and power of Jesus and was gloriously set free. She chose to serve and support Jesus as a result. We who are surrounded by temptations all the time in our *eros*-obsessed culture should learn the lesson of her testimony and mine. There's a dreadful payback for sexual sin. It is not harmless fun. It is much better to listen to our consciences at the enticement stage than to have to experience the agony of entrapment.

A Terrible Searing

There's not enough talk about the human conscience any more. It seems that we have almost forgotten that we have one. This is exceedingly dangerous. Our conscience is our moral compass. If we don't use it, if we allow it to be destroyed, we shouldn't be surprised if we find ourselves shipwrecked.

When the cycle of addiction begins to kick in, there is a season in which we can listen to the voice of our consciences and submit to God's Word and his will. While our consciences are receptive to the Holy Spirit, we need to follow through in obedience, however radical and counter-cultural that may seem. If we do not our consciences may eventually become so seared that we reach the point of no return.

This is what Paul tells his spiritual son Timothy. Paul mentored Timothy, teaching him how to watch both what he believed and how he behaved. In both respects, Paul wanted Timothy to honour Jesus. Let's have a look at the passage in context: 'The Spirit clearly says that in later times some will abandon the faith and follow deceiving spirits and things taught by demons. Such teachings come through hypocritical liars, whose consciences have been seared as with a hot iron' (1 Timothy 4:1-2).

Paul prophesies that in the future a great danger will arise in the church. Christians will abandon their trust in God and his Word and will turn to follow 'deceiving spirits' and 'things taught by demons'. The people responsible for this deception will have had their consciences seared as with a hot iron.

How does somebody 'turn to follow' deceiving spirits?

Does it mean people will catch a glimpse of a ghost beckoning them and follow after it?

Will they see a giant bed sheet which spookily exerts a magnetic draw to those it wants to entice with the promise of something seductive?

Will leprechauns appear with a fake roadmap to the nearest pot of gold?

Is this what Paul meant by deceiving spirits?

It all seems a bit far-fetched.

What about 'things taught by demons'? Really?

Does Paul envisage groups of Christians secretly attending an evening class led by the local demonic fraternity? Do they sit taking notes as goblin-like creatures conduct seminars and lectures? Or does Paul mean something less obvious than that? Could it be that those who are deceived by these 'eebie jeebies' aren't even aware of what is going on? Could it be that they're under the impression that what they come to believe is purely the product of human insight and has no supernatural root whatsoever?

The Bible says of those who promote lies and deception that they have allowed their 'consciences to become seared as with a hot iron'. Their sensitivity to their consciences has been numbed by repeated sinful behaviour. Things that initially made them flinch and wince, have long ago stopped giving them any level of concern. By succumbing to the pressure put on them by these shadows, they have been pulled into the cycle of addiction, and they are now too entrapped to tell truth from lies, the light from the darkness.

Before my breakthrough moment, I would have felt that, while admittedly I was on this cycle, at least I was not 'too far' along it. I think my perception would have been that I was in a normal place for a single, red-blooded male. Yet in retrospect I would have to acknowledge now that I was in a state of disobedience, a place which shadows could access and where strongholds could be established. Indeed, I can see that I was in a place of rebellion against God. It took my repeated lack of submission to God to bring me there, but if I'm honest with myself, the reality is that I was there.

In terms of my sex life, this is how I spent eighteen years in a state of spiritual revolt making myself at home at that popular resort called the Costa del Rebellion.

Let me paint a picture for you:

GOD NUDGES ME...

Don't watch this TV show or movie it will affect you badly—I watch it anyway.

Don't flick through the channels late at night—I flick through them anyway.

Don't search the internet for that thing that you're thinking of searching for—I search for it anyway.

Don't cross that sexual boundary with your girlfriend—I cross it anyway.

Don't masturbate, resist the urge to do it—I masturbate anyway.

Don't think about that person in a sexual way—I think about them anyway.

Consistently poor decisions resulted in increasing rebellion. Rebellious attitudes and sinful acts led to shadows and strongholds in my life.

Listen, the only way you can prevent this from happening is to listen to what the Holy Spirit is saying to your conscience as you read or listen to the Word of God.

What state, then, is your conscience in?

Is it alert to the promptings of God, guiding you?

Is it fully submitted to God?

Or has it already been seared?

Are you already in a place of compromise and rebellion?

Now is the time to trust God to help you change.

No Place for the Devil

The Bible says in Ephesians 4:27, 'neither give a place to the devil' (KJV). The word *place* literally means 'an inhabitable space'. The Greek word Paul uses is *topos*. This is the same word that is used when the Bible talks about Joseph and Mary looking for an available room in Bethlehem. Paul chooses this word here. He is exhorting his readers, 'don't give an inhabitable space to the enemy.' Make sure there is no room in the inn of your soul for the devil or his shadows.

'But hang on a minute', you reply, 'what happens if I do give a place to the enemy?' If we give him an inhabitable place, the devil will take it. He will say, 'Thank you very much', and move into every room of your heart. He will exert squatter's rights if you let him. Give him an inch, and he'll take a mile.

If you are still reading this and can see that you are moving from enticement to enactment, you need to take stock of your position. Listen to your conscience while it is receptive to God. Get down to repentance. This is critical if you are to avoid being controlled by a stronghold. Prevention is better than cure. The further you go down the cycle of addiction, the more difficult it becomes to backtrack.

My own story should serve as a warning. I look back on my descent into eventual entrapment with amazement now. How could I not see that for me to follow the pull to masturbate, look at pornography, and push sexual boundaries with members of the opposite sex outside of marriage was not the behaviour of a follower of Jesus? How had I become so numb that my heart was no longer broken by what I was doing?

There were times when I did glimpse reality, and I wanted so much to be free. However, the longer I continued to give in to sexual sin, the more I developed an appetite for it, and the less concerned I was at looking at more explicit things and pushing past physical boundaries.

There had been a time when I would feel remorse for taking a second look at a woman scantily clad on the front cover of a men's magazine as I walked past it on a news stand. There had been a time when I felt conviction from the Holy Spirit as I passionately kissed a girlfriend. Several years of compromise later, however, I would happily and regularly push sexual boundaries, not to mention seek out far more hardcore pornographic material in an attempt to satisfy an insatiable appetite. What initially was unthinkable to me became more acceptable as I travelled a slow journey of spiritual decay.

Looking back, I should have resisted right at the beginning when the devil was trying to get his foot in the door.

I should have said no to enticements while my conscience was still tender.

And so—if I may be bold—should you.

You still have a way out; take it now, before it's too late.

Don't give the devil any inhabitable space in your life.

Let Jesus be Lord of every room in your house, including the bedroom.

Any thoughts on this chapter? Participate in the conversation on ☙ twitter: @pfsbook #theslipperyslope or ⓕ www.facebook.com/pfsbook

CHAPTER 5

EXPLICIT WORSHIP

The water carrier approached the well at noon, beads of sweat forming on her brow. The sun's rays beat upon her head, furrowed under the weight of her clay water jar.

There's never anyone here at this hour, she thought.

She had planned it perfectly, as she always did. The other women from her village came to the well in the cooler hours of the early morning or evening. She came at noon, the hottest time of the day, when no one in their right minds bore the burden of a heavy load.

'I'd really like a drink.'

The voice startled her. She had been day dreaming.

'Pardon me?'

'I'd really be grateful for a drink,' the voice said calmly, courteously.

The woman looked at the man who had interrupted her solitude. He was sitting the other side of the well, exhausted and tired. He was clearly Jewish and dressed like a Rabbi. The tassels on his prayer shawl were frayed and dusty.

He shouldn't be talking to me. He should have removed himself twenty paces.

'Why are you asking me for a drink?' she scolded. 'I'm Samaritan scum, the lowest of the low, dirty from the cradle— at least according to you Jewish men.'

The woman placed her jar beside the well, getting ready to draw water.

The stranger looked at her with dark but warm eyes, the faintest trace of a smile on his face.

'I've got living water to offer you,' he said. 'It's so good, you'll never need to come back here to do this again. Trust me, it's heavenly.'

'What are you talking about?' the woman said. 'Where's your bucket? Where's this living water?'

'You drink from this well,' the stranger said, 'and you'll be thirsty again. You drink from my well, and you'll never be thirsty again.'

The woman put her hands on her hips and stared at him.

'Now you're just boasting.'

'Listen,' the stranger said, 'you accept my offer and you'll discover a spring in the centre of your heart, one that overflows with water every day—the water of life, real life, eternal life.'

The woman's scowl disappeared.

Her eyes glistened like the shimmering water in the well.

'I don't know who you are,' she said, 'but please give me some of this water. I really don't want to keep coming back here. It's so hot. And I'm so, so tired.'

The stranger smiled.

'Go back to the village and bring your husband,' he said. 'This is for both of you.'

'The woman looked down at the sand.

'I don't have a husband,' she replied.

The stranger paused, his eyes meeting hers as she looked up momentarily.

'That's true,' he whispered. 'But it's also true that you've had five husbands and you're living with a man who's not your husband.'

The woman grabbed her dress, startled, gripping tightly to the fabric, almost tearing it with her worn fingernails.

How did he know that?

Suddenly she realised.

'You're obviously a prophet, sir,' she stuttered, 'a Jewish prophet at that. Us Samaritans and you Jews, well, we have different beliefs. Samaritans worship on Mount Gerazim over there. You Jews say it's got to be in Jerusalem.'

'It doesn't have to be in Jerusalem,' the stranger said.

'What?' the woman exclaimed.

'The important thing is not where you worship but who you worship, and how.'

'What does that mean?'

'It means that God is not remote, he's relational. And he's not looking for slaves; he's looking for sons and daughters.'

'But how can that be?'

'Because God is the Father you've been waiting for all your life.'

A tear ran quickly down the woman's sunburned cheek.

'Daughter,' the man said, 'you've been looking for love in all the wrong places. These men you've been with cannot satisfy you. Only your Heavenly Father can. He alone can quench your need for intimacy. Believe me.'

The woman was crying now.

I need this so bad.

'Worship your Heavenly Father,' the stranger said. 'That's where you'll find the answer—in his arms, not in the arms of other men.'

As he spoke these words, something began to emerge from the depths of the woman's spirit—a heart cry, a visceral cry, a silent primal cry.

Daddy!

'He's looking for daughters like you,' the stranger said. 'His hug is better than any hug you've ever had.'

'When the Messiah comes,' she stammered, 'he'll tell us about all this stuff.'

The stranger stood to his feet.

'I,' he said, 'I am he.'

The woman was running now, away from the well. Back towards the town—heart thumping, legs pumping.

I've got to tell everyone he's here.

She had left the water jar at the cusp of the old well.

The stranger never got his drink.

But she had.

It's All about Worship

If that story sounds familiar to you it's because it's from the Gospels—from John chapter 4 to be specific. And it's a great introduction to this chapter on explicit worship because it showcases how Jesus understands worship. In his view, worship is the intimate and adoring affection of a son or a daughter towards the most perfect, loving heavenly Father. It is what every human being needs to discover.

The truth is we are all of us hardwired to worship. The problem is that if we don't direct our worship drive towards the Creator, we will end up directing it towards the created, just like the Samaritan woman did. Even the original language in this story highlights this. The word Jesus would have used for husband is *baal*. Does that sound familiar? Baal was an ancient Canaanite god who became an idol to the Israelites.

The woman's root issue was therefore one of idolatry. She was worshipping men. She had become addicted to sexual relationships with one man after another. She was looking in men for what she could only find in her heavenly Father. She was idolising her *baalim* rather than her *Abba* (a word meaning 'Papa,' Dad,' 'Daddy', 'Dearest Father').

Consequently she was always thirsty and never satisfied. Until, that is, she encountered Jesus.

The Worship of Pleasure

What or whom do you idolise? What are you deeply into? Is there something that has shifted from being a guilty pleasure to an idol? Many of us are bowing down to something every single day. At which altar do you worship?

Worship is defined in the dictionary as *the reverent love and devotion accorded a deity, an idol or a sacred object.*

Reverential love and devotion are not things offered only to 'God'. We can just as readily pour our affection and dedication into something else with equal or indeed greater enthusiasm—something that becomes an idol.

We can, for example, be quickly sucked into the black hole of hedonism—or the worship of pleasure. Idolatry and hedonism are actually very close to one another; they are twin cities sharing the same skyline. We start with an inquisitive mind, searching out fulfilment of an appetite or an instinct. We desire something, so we allow ourselves to partake of it. This hedonistic pursuit shifts gear, seamlessly becoming what the Bible labels 'idolatry'.

'I said to myself, "Come now, I will test you with
pleasure. So enjoy yourself." ...all that my eyes desired, I
did not refuse them. I did not withhold my heart from
any pleasure, for my heart was pleased because of all my
labour and this was my reward for all my labour.'

(Ecclesiastes 2:1-11—NASB)

Solomon's words in Ecclesiastes reveal that his heart had tipped over into hedonism. His journey to Pleasureville may appeal to us on a surface level, but 700 wives (not to mention 700 mothers-in-law), 300 concubines and a billion dollar bank account later, it was apparent to everyone around him that Solomon's approach to life had caused him to really lose the plot. For Solomon, the wives, the bits on the side, and the idea that anything he wanted was fair game, was the catalyst for his demise. While he was offering himself totally to these things, it incrementally became an act of worship.

Exactly the same thing can happen to you and me. When we sit in front of a computer and pleasure ourselves while watching our five-minute fantasy, we are erecting an idol at the altar of pornography.

Offering our bodies sexually is accordingly far deeper than just a physical act. Sexual relationships, pornography and lust are in reality acts of worship. We may not physically bow down in an act of worship, but our worship is evident by our obsession, investment and fetish. As Peter Horrobin rightly says, 'all sexual expression is an act of worship, whether the participants are aware of this fact or not. Some marriage services contain the vows, "With my body, I thee worship".'

Having your 'Kate' and 'Edith'

When you worship an idol like sex, it does not necessarily follow that you will stop worshipping Jesus. In biblical history, the Israelites never completely abandoned the worship of

God (Yahweh). But they did 'add on' the worship of gods like Baal to their existing worship. This combination of various contradictory belief systems is called syncretism. The worship of Baal was in direct contravention of God's Law, yet they did it anyway. They wanted to have their cake and eat it.

One way Baal worship was practised was by both male and female temple prostitutes carrying out sex acts which would apparently arouse Baal who would then bring rain causing 'mother earth' to be fertile. Rather than rely on God for everything, the people of Israel incorporated these unhealthy practices in order to get the best of both worlds. They worshipped Baal and Yahweh simultaneously. Though they did not realise it, the practice of Baal worship was actually invoking dark demonic forces. This is the reality of idolatry.

I believe that Baal worship and generic syncretism have the same spiritual implications. I can justify my choices of sexual proclivity by labelling them as an 'alternative lifestyle choice'. Similarly I can convince myself that it is an out-dated version of Christianity that sees premarital or extramarital 'sexual expression' as compromise. In order to express my submerged desires, I indulge in a modernised version of syncretism. I 'add on' my desired extras to supplement my Christianity. This is pick and mix Christianity.

The truth remains that, though you may not be consciously worshipping Baal, you are still not able to separate yourself from the detrimental spiritual consequences of sexual behaviour. You are worshipping something, and, like the people of Israel as they committed idolatry, you have no control over what is being invoked by your decisions.

It is for this reason that the Apostle Paul is so adamantly opposed to those in Corinth who were also trying to have their cake and eat it—to have a 'pick n' mix' Christianity. Listen to what he says in 2 Corinthians 6:14-18. In a passage entitled 'Warning Against Idolatry' (NIV), Paul tells the church not to be 'yoked together with unbelievers.' Light and darkness can have no fellowship with one another. So don't sleep with temple prostitutes. Don't be yoked sexually with pleasure-worshippers. You become fixated on these things and it will affect your spiritual life in an extremely destructive way, for 'what agreement is there between the temple of God and idols?' Christians are not to commit idolatry with their bodies because their bodies are temples of the living God. Therefore Paul writes, 'come out and separate yourself from these things.' God wants to be a Father to you, and for you to be his intimate sons and daughters. Worship him not idols.

The Naughty Gnostics Rise Again

How is it that we can so easily put physical, sexual acts into one compartment and our spiritual lives in another? How can we separate these things and allow them to co-exist without it affecting us? Is there wrong thinking we have embraced to permit such a strange contradiction?

The answer is yes.

Most likely we have unwittingly embraced a system of thought known as Gnosticism, after the Greek word *gnosis* meaning 'knowledge.' This system is effectively one which prides itself on superior enlightenment. It was a virus that infected the church in the first century. It is a virus that is infecting the church in the twenty first century too.

Although the strains of this virus varied, and indeed morphed, Gnosticism was extremely prevalent for the first couple of centuries after Christ and it caused a lot of damage to the early church. I'm not going to attempt to explain the complexities of this philosophical system in any detail because I could not do it justice, but in its basic sense Gnosticism held to the idea that 'spirit' is good and 'matter' is evil. Therefore it is the spiritual realm that's important. The physical and material realm is worthless.

People who embraced this Gnostic way of thought believed that whatever is done in the physical body, however depraved, has no negative impact because life exists in the realm of the 'spirit' only. This idea then justified sinful behaviour, especially sexual behaviour—because sexual acts are obviously physical. In the Gnostic mindset, they therefore don't matter and have no impact on our spiritual lives.

The naughty Gnostics, it is fair to say, have re-emerged in our own time and their thinking has empowered those following 'alternative' lifestyles. Gnostic thinking has also even led some to believe that they can evolve to higher levels of spiritual insight through sexual expression. This kind of folly has its root in the dualism at the foundations of Gnostic thought. People truly buy into the notion that what they do in the body does not affect them in terms of their spirit. This is flawed thinking indeed.

I had unconsciously taken Gnostic thinking and attitudes on board in my own life before my deliverance. I was prepared to believe that my spiritual life was okay despite my decisions to express myself sexually through relationships and pornography. I had made a 'matter' and 'spirit' distinction. I had not consciously embraced the Gnostic ideology but it had certainly begun to infiltrate my worldview. Indeed, this ideology had become a 'stronghold'—an unbiblical, demonic ideology that had a strong hold over my thinking.

Since my deliverance, however, I see things very differently.

I cannot worship both my heavenly Father and sexually immoral behaviours.

I cannot separate my spiritual life from these unlawful, physical acts.

And I cannot accept the deceptive lie that says that what I do in my body has no spiritual implications.

Sexual sin damages us in our spiritual life, and indeed in every part of our lives—our emotions, minds, memories, imaginations, everything.

Don't Idolise a Partner

All this shows how important it is to worship the Creator not the created. The Samaritan woman worshipped men. That was idolatry. She had to be reoriented from the creature to the Creator. She had to realise that idolising men was not the answer. Worshipping the Father in intimate adoration was her only hope. It was in the Father's arms that her love hunger was truly going to be met.

This brings me to an important final point about worship. *Don't idolise a partner.*

We have to admit that love can sometimes turn into idolatry. For many people, the intensity of a relationship can quickly cause dependency, and this can happen unknowingly over time. When this happens, it becomes of far greater importance for us to lean on that relationship than it is to lean on God. In a word, that's 'idolatry.'

In its rightful, God-ordained context, worship is something that our spirit does through our body. At a church service, or in the privacy of our homes, our spirit is filled with the desire to connect with God and worship him. Our bodies are then involved in this act of worship; we may raise our hands and we will certainly use our voices. In this respect, the adoration in our spirits overflows into the actions of our bodies.

In addition our emotions have a part to play. Our souls are stirred as we feel God's presence. When this happens, joy floods our hearts, and a sense of the love and peace of God invades our human emotions. In true worship, the whole of our being is therefore involved. It is not just an act that involves our spirits. It also involves our bodies and souls.

The same is true when we worship the created instead of the Creator. When this happens, our partner displaces God. We experience a deep longing for that person which is stronger than our longing for God. As soon as that happens, the seeds of idolatry have already been planted. Then we begin to express our worship of that person through our hands and our voices, just as in the worship of God. And in all of this our emotions are not unaffected. We sense the counterfeit of lasting joy which is momentary pleasure, the counterfeit of true peace which is fleeting contentment, the counterfeit of holy love which is ephemeral *eros*.

We should therefore never idolise a partner.

In marriage, we should love our spouse in a unique, exclusive and self-giving way.

But we should never turn our spouse into an idol.

It says in Romans 11.36, 'to him be the glory forever' (NASB).

Who is Paul referring to?

He is referring to God Almighty.

Only God deserves our worship.

To him alone should be given glory—that is, 'pre-eminence.'

After hearing a minister preach on the Second Coming of Christ, Queen Victoria famously said: 'I wish he would come during my lifetime so that I could take my crown and lay it at his feet'.

Now that's what I'm talking about.

Our 'crown', whatever that may be, must be laid down. Queen Victoria understood this all too well. Even for royalty, or the rich and famous, the glory belongs to God. His pre-eminence is supreme.

When our worship is directed toward God, it has found its perfect expression, but when we fix our worship on other things, we have blemished the intended blueprint given by God. We are resonating with an imperfect cadence, and we are out of tune.

Maybe like me, you have, in your time, put a relationship in the place of glory. You have given a person pre-eminence. For you, they have become the most important thing. They are over and above God. They hold the position of glory.

C. S. Lewis, in his book *The Weight of Glory*, says it this way: 'Our Lord finds our desires not too strong but too weak. We're half-hearted creatures, fooling around with drink and sex and ambition. When infinite joy is offered us, like an ignorant child who wants to go on making mud pies in a slum, because he cannot imagine what is meant by the offer of a holiday at the sea. We are far too easily pleased'.

We settle for sin at the expense of the glory that God would offer us in his presence. Pornography, masturbation, premarital and extramarital sex are the mud pies that we favour instead. I could have had intimacy with God, but instead I chose nudity, rebellion and sin.

C. S. Lewis says, 'We are far too easily pleased'. How right he is.

All of us can find ourselves like the Samaritan woman, worshipping our imperfect partners, whoever they are.

When Jesus arrived, she found perfection.

She moved from worshipping men to worshipping God.

It is through an encounter with Jesus that our idols can be confronted and destroyed.

It is through him that we can turn our affections away from the created to the Creator.

Don't choose dirty water from rusty cisterns.

Choose living water.

The Stranger from Heaven is offering it to you.

Any thoughts on this chapter? Participate in the conversation on 🐦 twitter: @ pfsbook #explicitworship or ◼ www.facebook.com/pfsbook

CHAPTER 6

CHEAP THRILLS AT A HIGH PRICE

The theme of this book is quite simple: there is a price to pay for our momentary, illicit pleasures. The experiences that come as a result of our choices to fulfil sexual stimuli in an unbiblical way don't come cheap.

In the Book of Proverbs, Solomon describes how cheap thrills enjoyed in the throes of sexual passion have a premium attached to them.

Keep from your neighbour's wife,
from the smooth talk of a wayward woman.

Do not lust in your heart after her beauty
or let her captivate you with her eyes.

For a prostitute can be had for a loaf of bread,
but another man's wife preys on your very life

(Proverbs 6:24-26—TNIV)

If you're single, have you ever had the 'hots' for another man's wife? Maybe you're on the other side of the equation. Though 'happily married' at least on paper, the reality is that your dissatisfaction with your life and your wife have sent you looking for greener grass. Even if you met her online, the woman you're lusting after is still 'your neighbour's wife'.

Maybe your fantasy of an evergreen relationship is just an idea occasionally referred to and then replaced in the filing cabinet of your mind. You have nonchalantly pulled out the photo and considered the possibility. Or maybe you have signed up to a website to look for 'friends' who will understand your marital disharmony. You find yourself casually clicking your way through the profiles—potential upgrades in the showroom. The new model is looking sportier and sexier than anything your wife has offered and the salesman speaking to you is making it very difficult to say no. You know the cost is more than you can afford but it is impossible to resist.

For some of you the journey has already begun. You took off your wedding ring, you arranged a meeting, you held her, you kissed her and you slept with her. Adultery is not a grey area; you are either doing it or not doing it. It's not worth trying to sugar-coat our behaviour. Let's call a spade a spade, especially when with full knowledge and intent we have used that spade to dig our own graves. Your neighbour's wife may have all the curves in all the right places. Equally, in your eyes, your own wife may be a relative disappointment. Your thought process is simple. The spouse you are now married to is distinctly different from the one whom you signed for and accepted delivery of on your wedding day. You didn't imagine marriage would look like this. You have had enough of the mood swings and the relentless nagging. It's time to 'ctrl, alt and delete' your way out of this. There was a time when you said, 'For better and for worse'—so much for that old adage now.

'keep... from the smooth talk of a wayward woman'

For some the 'smooth talk' referred to here was enough to tear you away from your commitment to monogamy and marriage. The inflation of your ego by one woman resulted in the deflation of your commitment to another. The Bible is clear about the costs and implications of 'playing away'. In terms of monetary expense, 'a loaf of bread' or the price of a meal in a restaurant can finance the physical experience that you crave. You can choose to pay for sex or take someone out for dinner, but does the payment really end there? Or will your whole life be devoted to paying off the extortionate APR? Make sure you look carefully at the quote and examine the invoice. Is the thrill you had in mind worth the bill you will need to pay?

Can a man scoop fire into his lap
without his clothes being burned?

Can a man walk on hot coals
without his feet being scorched?

So is he who sleeps with another man's wife;
no one who touches her will go unpunished
(Proverbs 6:27-29)

Yes, the woman you're looking at is hot, but so is hell! If you decide to engage in intimacy with someone you are not married to (figuratively speaking, scoop hot coals into your lap), it will be hot. You may even for a few short moments enjoy it, but be under no illusion, it will hurt. You cannot spend any length of time on a red-hot surface without experiencing burns and blisters. Once your feet have been injured this badly, you will have to spend the rest of your life living with the scars that have been formed. The pain and scarring that we are discussing will be yours if you choose to sin sexually. If you touch a woman that is not your wife, you choose to etch that decision permanently into your soul. It becomes a permanent artefact on the mantle of your moral inventory.

People do not despise a thief if he steals
to satisfy his hunger when he is starving.

Yet if he is caught, he must pay sevenfold,
though it costs him all the wealth of his house.

But a man who commits adultery has no sense;
whoever does so destroys himself
(Proverbs :30-32)

This verse opens by highlighting the identification that each of us would feel with the thief who steals to satisfy his hunger. What can a man do when he is starving? He has to eat! If it means somebody else can't eat, then so be it. The survival of the fittest is the route to a satisfied stomach. We eat to meet our own physical needs. In our own framework of justice, we would forgive a hungry man a multitude of things. But this verse makes an interesting comparison. It asks us to compare the physical hunger pangs of the thief with the sexual ones of an adulterer. Is the appetite of a man for sex as justifiable as his appetite for food and drink?

Why is it that we can be equally or indeed more aroused by a porn star engaging in the nastiest kind of sex as we can by our own wife? In the mind of a man driven by lust, sex is sex. If it stimulates me, it needs to be fulfilled. This mindset is equivalent to that of a toddler crawling along a dirty pavement. The kid has no discernment about what they eat; they put EVERYTHING in their mouths. One day that baby will draw a clear distinction between a random banana skin decaying next to the faecal matter of a rodent, and a gourmet meal at a 5-star restaurant. Unfortunately, immaturity means that both of these things are currently equally appealing.

We need to learn that we are not to put everything in our mouths. Toddlers confusedly consider anything that could be edible as food, and this is what happens when we start to pursue sexual contact outside of marriage, as opposed to cherishing sexual union within it. You can eat what you're looking at, but you will develop a permanent stomach ache.

Both theft and adultery have a high price. Firstly, let's look at the hungry thief mentioned in this verse. He would have to compensate for what he had taken and this would be expensive. Apparently he would have to '*pay sevenfold, though it costs him all the wealth of his house*' for whatever he took. This is high interest indeed.

But the cost of adultery is even greater. In the verse above, the high price of our cheap thrill becomes clear. The Bible says that *whoever does so destroys himself*. Our decisions to follow the guidance of our sexual compass can bring destruction to our entire life. A holistic wipe-out of emotional, spiritual and, potentially, physical health through bondage, baggage and disease is entirely possible.

Thank God for Jesus and the totality of his work at Calvary which bring us back in alignment with our 'true north'.

An Alternative Lifestyle

What is the answer to the short-lived fulfilment of cheap thrills? Is there any realistic alternative? Yes, there is a far more sustainable solution that will bring unparalleled satisfaction in a completely different realm to the gratification we are used to. It's called holiness!

Are you married? Are you single? Are you 'in a relationship'? If you fit any of these characteristics, and if you love Jesus, I implore you to commit yourself to a life of holy living. I beg you to make the choice today—a choice not to be involved sexually with anybody until the day you get married. Join me in the decision to wait for a day when a righteous validation and expression of your sexuality can happen. Please wait for the covenant of marital union rather than the carnal instinctive and sensual channels that would be your current means of expression. Holiness is God's plan for you.

Let's be specific. What do I mean by being 'involved sexually'? I fervently believe that this definition includes any act that creates, enhances and stimulates sexual desire in one or more of the persons involved. It includes kissing, touching and even flirtation. Any of these things are at their root foreplay, and they are all about the preparation of the body for sex. For me my commitment to holiness involves abstaining from these things until the day I get married (if I ever do). I am convinced that, in terms of sexuality, this is what holiness looks like and I truly believe it is totally within our reach.

The Bible says, 'be holy; without holiness no one will see the Lord' (Hebrews 12:14). Holiness is not subjective. It is not a variant dependent upon opinion, 'user experience' or sexual drive. There are two options—holiness and sinfulness. Genuine Christianity will eventually affect the sex life of the believer. If you haven't arrived yet, don't lose heart and think that you can't achieve it.

The Price has been Paid

We have explored the reality that cheap thrills come at a high price. For many, the mindset is that holiness comes at an equally high price. It's true the price of holiness is high. But what really is the cost? Celibacy, misery, unfulfilment and the sacrifice of sexual and emotional expression are, contrary to popular belief, not the price of holiness. The price is actually much greater than that.

What is it? What is the price? It's called the blood of Jesus. Jesus paid the price for us to become holy. We couldn't become truly holy through our self-efforts, however arduous and impressive. The truth is, only the blood of Jesus could deal effectively and permanently with our sin. It was through his death that the price for holiness was paid. Holiness is not achieved through our effort but through Christ's.

The blood of Jesus therefore means that we have access, should we choose to take advantage of it, to the divine nature. So stop trying to be holy in your own strength. Receive the benefits of the perfect work achieved by Jesus. Choose holiness and receive his empowering grace. Sooner or later it will take effect in your life and you will be holy, as he is holy.

Remember this: holiness is not achieved by our immense effort and endeavour. It is a combination of receiving more and more grace and making right choices.

We should therefore aim to live lives that reflect the holiness of God. Holiness is not some religious, fictional tale. It really does exist. Receive it today by faith and move forward.

Any thoughts on this chapter? Participate in the conversation on twitter: @pfsbook #cheapthrills or www.facebook.com/pfsbook

CHAPTER 7

BONDAGE—
BUT NOT WHAT I HAD IN MIND

Sorry to disappoint you. There will be no mention of whips or S & M. Handcuffs do get a mention though!

In that dark phase of my life when sexual attachments, pornography and masturbation had a prominent position on the stage of my private life, I was thinking about bondage—but not about bondage. I jest not; my focus was on sexual gratification, not on spiritual slavery.

Today I would say that the two are inseparable.

You get obsessed with gratifying the sexual appetites of your body and you'll become bound like a slave in your spirit.

Bondage and bondage are the same.

It's just that people don't realise it.

That's the theme of this chapter.

Don't be an Ass

In the Gospels we read about an encounter between a crippled woman and Jesus:

'...and a woman was there who had been crippled by a spirit for eighteen years. She was bent over and could not straighten up at all. When Jesus saw her, he called

her forward and said to her, "Woman, you are set free from your infirmity." Then he put his hands on her, and immediately she straightened up and praised God.'

(Luke 13:11-12)

Jesus goes on to say the following:

'Doesn't each of you on the Sabbath untie his ox or donkey from the stall and lead it out to give it water? Then should not this woman, a daughter of Abraham, whom Satan has kept bound for eighteen long years, be set free on the Sabbath day from what bound her?'

In this passage, Luke is relaying an incident where Jesus has healed a woman with a major back or spinal issue. Jesus goes on to give a very telling analogy, comparing her affliction to an animal being tied to a post in a stall.

Jesus explains that a donkey can only be taken to water if it has been unfastened from the place where it was tied. The unrelenting midday sun may be beating hard on that donkey's back, and the donkey may be dangerously dehydrated and desperately thirsty, but unless the rope is untied and the animal led to water, it will not be able to satisfy its thirst. The donkey is not itself capable of breaking away from what ties it. Despite straining to reach the bucket of water just beyond its reach, the rope around its neck prevents it from drinking. The animal is not fully aware of the reason for its inability to move. It just knows it can't.

Equally, we don't know what had caused this woman to become tied to this condition, but this detail doesn't matter. The point is, no matter what we are tied to, we can be separated and untied from it.

The woman in this account was probably not certain why she could not stand straight. She may have had multiple diagnoses and endured many attempts to prescribe medication. But Jesus simply says that the woman had been bound by Satan for eighteen years. He saw what her real need was and he set her free.

Cutting Invisible Ties

One of the most important aspects of Jesus' ministry is to untie the invisible cords that hold us captive and to set us free in every possible area of life and experience.

Jesus isn't just concerned that we receive his forgiveness. He is just as passionate about us receiving his freedom.

Too many Christians are forgiven but they're not free.

They are still tied up, like a donkey.

There are numerous ways in which we can find ourselves tied up and held back from drinking living water and living God's best. We can be affected by unresolved issues such as deep-rooted habits, past relationships or emotional instability. This may be your experience: you feel deep bitterness just at the mention of the name of somebody you haven't had any contact with for years. It may be that on some level you still feel connected to a person you had a romantic relationship with long ago.

Such things may have left a negative imprint on you. This imprint then causes you to live in fear or bitterness. These wounds need to be dealt with. We need the tethers and ties cut in our emotions. Indeed, we should expect to have complete freedom in every area of life—freedom that lasts and leaves no trace of bondage, including in our emotions.

Some of my fondest childhood memories involve trips with my dad to the local river where we enjoyed some father and son time while fishing. These trips together certainly strengthened our bond. We would spend hours on the River Lee attempting to catch a monster fish. I was fascinated with fishing. I loved every minute of it (except the moments when my dad caught more or larger fish than I did!).

Think about what was going on under the water while we were waiting for a bite. Wiggling on a hook at the end of my line was a cocktail of maggots—an appetising meal to tempt a fish. As these fish caught sight of their potential dinner, they were oblivious of the fact that this tasty meal was embedded on a razor-sharp, barbed hook attached to an invisible line. The fish was unaware that beyond its field of vision another world existed where humans roamed, longing to catch them.

When the fish took the bait, it was suddenly connected to the invisible line. This line pulled them towards an unknown source—a person trying to trap them. They had no idea that this was going on. They tried to resist the line for a while but in the end they had to capitulate.

What a picture! This is precisely what's happening in the spiritual realm when we take the bait of sexual temptation. We must learn to discern what is happening when the enemy presents his fishing tackle. We need to remember that snacking on maggots will result in bondage.

Getting Hooked

If we imagine ourselves for a moment as members of the fishy world, we can see how the enemy entices us as a fisherman entices a fish. It is easy to see how pornography is more than it initially appears to be and yet how the bait of the enemy can be so enticing. Like fish, naturally appealing images are dangling right in front of our eyes. Tasty maggots look like the perfect meal. How can we resist?

When fish see a worm on a hook, their natural instinct is to eat it. As Christians, however, we need to use discernment so that we recognise the concealed hooks and the invisible lines used by the enemy to catch us. In terms of our sexuality, it is not that we are never supposed to enjoy a tasty meal. We are, but within the covenant of marriage. Until we are married, we are not to get hooked. We are to steer clear of the enemy's bait.

Sometimes a specific traumatic experience can cause us to become tethered and bound.

Let me give you an example from my personal experience.

In March 2011 I was riding my Vespa back home from a meeting. I was the only person travelling on my side of the road. In the distance I saw a black BMW on the other side. It was travelling at about 70mph and progressively increasing in speed. As it drew closer, it veered from its side of the road and was now almost completely on my side. To my horror, I saw it was on a collision course with me! As I realised this, I immediately slowed down and pulled into the kerb in an attempt to get out of its way. The BMW adjusted its angle to compensate for my adjustment and increased its speed. It was now travelling at 90mph.

My heart was pounding, and a sense of panic and fear overtook me. I honestly felt that this was it; the car was going to hit me. In movie-like fashion, at the very last second the approaching vehicle screeched away from me, finally swerving and adjusting its course. It then accelerated past me and sped into the distance on the correct side of the road.

This was among the most traumatic and terrifying moments of my life. Afterwards, I was physically shaking and trying to control my racing heart. I was freaked out. I eventually regained composure and drove back home.

Have you ever genuinely experienced déjà vu? Well let me tell you about my experience. Three weeks after my encounter with the BMW, I was driving down the same road when, to my astonishment, the same car, following the same trajectory, drove towards me at the same speed. That same sense of fear flooded my body all over again; it was tangible. It was extremely frightening, but then, unlike the last time it happened, right before the moment of impact, I woke up. I was sitting bolt upright, and I realised that I had actually dreamed it.

The events that had happened to me three weeks earlier had now recurred in a dream. As I sat in my bed nursing my pounding heart, I took a few deep breaths and eventually lay down, rolled over, and went back to sleep. During the course of the night that same dream was repeated in exact detail four times in a row. Each time I woke up sitting upright in fear. I always woke up at the exact moment of impact, and I was always sitting bolt upright. I'm a little bit slow so it wasn't until the fourth repetition of the dream that I realised what was going on. I saw this dream for what it was. I got out of my bed and I started to pray. I prayed against fear and against its effects in my life. I spoke directly to any shadow of fear that had been attempting to affect me since this 'near miss' three weeks earlier. I was very serious; I was in a warfare zone. I repeated the words of Paul to Timothy, affirming the scripture:

God hath not given us the spirit of fear; but of power, and of love, and of a sound mind.

(2 Timothy 1:7—KJV)

I prayed for about twenty minutes and then I felt that whatever had been burdening me was lifted. It was now 5 a.m., and I climbed back into bed and went to sleep. That dream has never been repeated since that day.

Tied by Trauma

I personally believe that in the heightened moment of fear during that 'near miss', the enemy had managed to tie a rope around me. He'd managed to latch onto my emotion of fear without me even knowing it. How did this happen? It actually didn't seem fair. I was not the one responsible for the near miss. The driver of the black BMW was.

As I reflected on this event, it began to annoy me. Why had a shadow attached to something for which I was not responsible? My involvement had been purely reactive and was a natural response to danger. Nonetheless the heightened emotions engendered by this near miss had given the enemy an opportunity to tie me up—just like that donkey we mentioned at the beginning of the chapter. I was temporarily bound by fear and it had affected me deeply. Thank God it only took a couple of weeks for this shadow to be highlighted and dealt with. Left unaddressed, that same shadow could have festered and given me some more serious problems.

This is an example of how bondages can happen even when it's not directly your fault. Maybe a shadow has latched onto something from your past—some trauma for which you were not responsible. Perhaps you have been the victim of sexual abuse or emotional abuse. Perhaps the death of a family member or close friend has left you emotionally paralysed. It was not your fault, something you couldn't control, something that was done to you. The devil found a way to affect you through a trauma like this, and you were not even aware that he was the one responsible for your subsequent torment.

Like me—after I woke up from that dream for the fourth time—you can now engage this shadow in the knowledge of what it is and what its purpose has been. Don't allow it to continue to affect you. Tackle it head on and, like me, walk in the freedom that God wants to give you.

Hidden Cords

Looking back, it is clear to me that I was unaware of the way my sexual bondage had led me into spiritual slavery.

Today I now realise that such a loss of freedom can happen in at least one of two ways. The first way I call 'invited' bondage. The second way I call 'inherited' bondage. Invited bondage is where we choose to tie ourselves to a post through sexually immoral acts. Inherited bondage is where other people tie us to a post through their acts—whether those acts come in the form of sexual abuse or dangerous driving.

Either way we end up in a form of spiritual slavery—whether it is through the heightened, harmful emotions caused by the traumatic things done to us, or through the intense, destructive thrill caused by the immoral things done by us.

It would serve us well to look carefully at what could be affecting us. We can fail to see the hidden cords that have entangled us. But we desperately need to be free and by God's grace we can be.

The following chapters will help you find out how this freedom can be received and enjoyed.

Any thoughts on this chapter? Participate in the conversation on 🐦 twitter: @pfsbook #nomorebondage or 📘 www.facebook.com/pfsbook

CHAPTER 8

EROGENOUS ZONES

In case you're not familiar with the term in my chapter title, here's the Wikipedia definition:

'An erogenous zone (from Greek *eros* "love" and *genous* "producing") is an area of the human body that has heightened sensitivity, the stimulation of which may result in the production of sexual fantasies or sexual arousal.'

Everything has its place and for married people reading this book, exploration of erogenous zones will form an important part of your physical relationship. When I talk about 'erogenous zones', however, my emphasis is on something else. Have patience; we will get to the juicy details shortly.

Good Eyesight

In the Sermon on the Mount (a passage of Scripture that is greatly loved but not greatly obeyed), Jesus said:

'The eye is the lamp of the body. If your eyes are healthy, your whole body will be full of light. But if your eyes are unhealthy, your whole body will be full of darkness. If then the light within you is darkness, how great is that darkness!'

(Matthew 6:22-23)

When talking about 'healthy eyes', Jesus was not referring to regular visits to Spec Savers. He was speaking figuratively and spiritually. He meant that our spiritual eyes are kept healthy by resisting the desire to look at things that are damaging to us. To take an obvious example, for the person addicted to pornography it is their eyes that are the problem. If they closed their eyes they would close the door in their souls to the darkness unleashed by pornographic images. Their eyes would then be healthy. But as soon as they open their eyes they open their souls. Once the door to their hearts is open, it's not just their eyes that become unhealthy. Their whole lives do too.

Looking at Trash

When we become stirred up and sexually aroused, it is often the result of looking at or listening to something inappropriate. We may look at a member of the opposite sex or at pornography, or we may allow our 'ears' to listen to seductive noises. On a purely natural level, these are often very appealing to our senses. Our 'erogenous zones' have been awakened. When we then act on these enticing sounds or sights, our hearts become contaminated by the dirty water funnelled through our eyes and ears.

One weekend several years ago, I opened my door to find something blocking it. A large plastic bag, completely full of books which were presumably intended for someone else, had been left outside my front door. I decided I would find out who these were for and get them back to them. I had a quick peek into the bag. It was full of Mills and Boon-style books— the worst kind of romantic trash, and raunchy romantic trash at that.

I took the bag into my room for 'safe keeping' and scanned several of the books. I also thumbed through the pages in search of some of the more overtly sexual passages. I then located the owner of the books and returned them. Chuckling to myself, I found it mildly amusing that someone I knew was a closet Mills and Boon fan (though I also had quite enjoyed what I'd read). Although I could hardly criticise a Mills and Boon fan when I was a porn watcher myself, I could see that these books were not just romantic but sexually explicit.

You may watch porn, or you may read romantic trash. I now realise that both of these things are on an equal par. Neither my neighbour nor I had any business reading trash or watching it. In reality, my eyes were gazing at darkness. I was in a world of shadows. I was a lead character in a real life trashy novel. I was "Christian Grey" and I was living out "shifty shades of Dave."

I did not have healthy eyes.

I was inviting shadows into my heart.

Enemy at the Gates

I made a covenant with my eyes not to look with lust at a young woman

(Job 31:1, NLT).

Job purposed in his heart that he would keep his eyes full of light and not look upon a woman lustfully. This is a great example, but by our own efforts it would be impossible to follow. However, with the help of the Holy Spirit we can accomplish it! It is not beyond our capacity.

We have two main channels into our mind. The seventeenth century author, John Bunyan, called them the Eye Gate and the Ear Gate. Pornography comes in through these gates. The gates of our eyes and ears are entrances to our soul and emotions.

We are ultimately responsible for what we let in through the gate of our emotions. If we become sloppy about our job as gatekeepers, potential trespassers are given a clear signal that their presence on our land is invited and welcomed. We should be sure that what we let in is wholesome and that its presence really is accepted and wanted.

I have had a variety of jobs over the years. One of the things I've done several times is tele-sales. Yes, I was one of those annoying people harassing you on the phone while you were in the middle of an evening meal.

During this phase I worked in publishing. One of my jobs was to sell advertising space. The goal was to find the person that controlled the purse strings. If you could speak to the decision maker and persuade them to allocate money from their marketing budget for advertising space in your magazine, it meant one thing ... commission!

The difficult part of this job was reaching the decision maker. These people are always hidden behind a protective ring of other staff members, and finally by the often impenetrable force of 'the gatekeeper'.

'Gatekeeper' is the name given by sales people to the personal assistant or secretary to the decision maker. The gatekeeper will always work extremely hard to protect the decision maker from unwanted phone calls. This necessitated extreme creativity. You would do what you had to do in order to connect with that person, even if it meant being 'economical with the truth.'

It was common practice to try to panic the gatekeeper into putting you through to the decision maker by exaggerating the urgency of the call. By adding words like 'critical' and 'time sensitive' to the conversation, or by making them think that they had forgotten about a pre-planned meeting, there was always a chance that you might be put through.

Why have I mentioned all of this?

I want us to understand how we are subject to similar processes in our thinking every day. We need to realise that our mind is the gatekeeper to a very critical decision maker, our will. Every day 'phone calls' are coming through to our minds, seeking to get the attention of our will. This means that we constantly need to operate a level of discernment to determine the validity of the 'call' coming through. Our job is to protect our decision maker from unnecessary conversations. We can actually block many of these conversations at an early stage before our decision maker even has to think about them. If we don't do this, unwanted calls from Mr. Depression or Ms. Lust will result in our marketing budget being spent on advertising space that is neither relevant nor helpful.

Watching our Motivation

If it's important to guard our minds, it's also just as important to guard our hearts.

We do this by being honest about our motivations.

So let me ask, is your motivation fully illuminated and pure when it comes to your sexuality?

In 1993 I had my first date. Several people from the church youth group went out with us, so fortunately I was not left alone. Had I been, I think I would have struggled to string a sentence together. I was so nervous.

About an hour into the event, something happened that, retrospectively, I find alarming. One of the guys in the group pulled me aside from the girl I was with. He was probably in his late teens and certainly in an influential position in my life.

'Dave,' he said, 'it looks like you might need one of these'.

He then took a pack of six condoms from his wallet. Tearing one from the ream, he handed it to me. Bearing in mind that I was thirteen years old and at that point had never been kissed, I didn't even know what this shiny square wrapper labelled 'extra large' was. After reading the wrapping, I was in a state of shock.

'Man, what are you doing?' I said to him. 'Why would I need that?'

He did not relent.

'You just never know,' he said, adding 'it's better to be safe than sorry.'

Looking back, the scary thing is that there was at least one guy in the church youth group who was anticipating an opportunity to use a condom. In fact he had at least five opportunities left in his wallet.

Maybe you are one of these Pentecostal playboys. It is actually not a laughing matter. Attending church with a packet of condoms in your back pocket is very dangerous. God will protect his daughters and you are on thin ice if you choose to play a gospel-gigolo game.

So scrutinise your motivations. Be ruthless.

Healthy Fixations

The Apostle Paul encouraged his readers to be careful about what they focused on with their eyes.

> So we fix our eyes not on what is seen, but on what
> is unseen. For what is seen is temporary, but what is
> unseen is eternal.

(2 Corinthians 4:18)

When we look at pornography or even give the obligatory ogle to an attractive girl in the office, we are actually looking at something temporary—a transient reality that will not remain. God has something so amazing projected in his vista for us but our eyes are fixed on pornographic images, temporary conquests, empty relationships and physical fulfilment. We have a lopsided focus. It is a fraction top-heavy on the physical rather than the spiritual.

The sad thing is, if you continue in the way you are going, your fixation may last until you're old and grey. Can you imagine the sad legacy left by our generation? A group of men exposed to the 'liberation' of free porn online remaining bound and unable to break free for a lifetime.

Porn addiction and masturbation does not stop when you get married. They cease when God sets you free.

Do you want to be seventy or eighty years old and still be a dirty old man looking at girls, the same age as your granddaughter, having sex?

How many will be living out this unfortunate reality, enjoying copulation on camera for a few moments of excitement?

Will you still be sitting in front of your computer with your genitals in your hand as an OAP?

Our erogenous zones were not created to be flooded with darkness. Instead they are to be filled with the light of God.

Let's not focus on looking at pornography or listening to alluring and destructive 'noises'. The God of creation needs to be our focus. With his help, we can transform our future and plot a new course to a land of healthy erogenous zones.

> Any thoughts on this chapter? Participate in the conversation on 🐦 twitter: @pfsbook #erogenouszones or
> 📘 www.facebook.com/pfsbook

CHAPTER 9

SEX ON THE BRAIN

The German Reformer, Martin Luther, once said, 'You can't stop birds flying past your head, but you can stop them from building a nest in your hair'.

Thoughts are like birds. Every day thoughts fly past us, and we decide whether to entertain those thoughts or reject them. Most people don't argue with their own thoughts; they take immediate ownership of them. These thoughts then come in for a landing and eventually build a nest to call home. The Bible is clear about the way we are supposed to deal with thoughts: 'take every thought captive and bring it to the obedience of Christ' (2 Corinthians 10:5—my paraphrase).

So when thoughts come into our minds, we should immediately grab them. Holding them in both hands, we can then consider their source. Is this something I am thinking? Is this something that God is saying to me? Or is this something coming from another source; i.e., is the devil injecting poison into my mind?

Thinking about Sex

I want to give you a few examples of the birds that the enemy sends to build nests in your hair. Consider the following species: jealousy, despair, rejection, hopelessness, self-pity, stress, lust and hatred. Do you recognise any of their feathers? This is just a small list from my own bespoke ornithology handbook.

On occasions, the strength of our own emotions can take us by surprise. They have a strong gravitational pull. We can be pulled into the orbit of self-pity or hopelessness very quickly. It might be that you feel like you frequently wake up under a dark cloud such as this. If that is the case, even if a nest has been almost completely built, there is nothing to stop you from taking that nest out, piece by piece, and trampling it under foot. That nest is not a flattering accoutrement. It is not your colour; it needs to go.

When it comes to lust, this nest is harbouring plenty of birds on plenty of heads. It's very possible yours is one of them. When it came to the nests in my hair, lust was certainly prominently positioned. Honestly speaking, I had sex on the brain.

I had always heard it said that men think about sex every seven seconds, though while trying to research this fact for the book I found nothing conclusive supporting it. However, I must admit to having thoughts about sex on a regular basis, certainly every couple of minutes. My habitual masturbation problem at the time was evidence that I was regularly thinking about sex and needed an outlet for my 'high sex drive'.

But was this abnormal? Is this not indicative of the male condition? Isn't thinking about sex simply intrinsic to the male mind? Surely science proves that the male libido is at this peak in order to keep the population of the species perpetuating. High sex drive is simply biology, or is it? Did God really programme us like that?

Contrary to popular belief, the great commandment is not, 'Go forth and multiply', but 'Love the Lord your God with all your heart, soul and mind.' God gives us an innate desire to love him over and above loving ourselves or indeed our partners. Our theology conquers our biology and our sexual desires eventually come into alignment with the 'divine nature' as we submit ourselves to him.

Where exactly does sex live? Is it on the brain, or is it in the heart? The answer to this question is both. It starts in the head and seeps into the heart by osmosis. You may genuinely believe that you don't have a 'problem'. But what does your private life have to say about this?

My own story is evidence that I was contaminated in heart, although I didn't know or understand it. Actually, my thinking and decision making were warped by a nest that had been firmly established on my head. I was half-man, half-nest!

Every day I was making choices to selfishly serve my own desires whether in an act of solo sex or a consenting sexual experience with a girlfriend or stranger at a party. Is this the normal Christian life?

Freedom is Possible

Despite all of the above, the truth is, a diluted conviction exists in spiritual people. Those once committed to fighting with determination will often eventually give up on the idea of holy living.

Are the hearts of men and women like me watered down out of disillusionment?

The Bible says, 'Hope deferred makes the heart sick' (Proverbs 13:12). What does this verse mean? It means that if a person hopes for something and this hope remains unfulfilled for a long time then eventually that person becomes disillusioned and gives up.

Unfulfilled expectations result in getting discouraged and rejecting holy living. This scripture in Proverbs sums up what is going on when these emotions arise. If we go with them, the ultimate destination is a heart that's sick.

Why are our expectations not met? Why is our hope of success in this area deferred? Is it because it is actually not possible to get disentangled from the grip of our sex drive? Or have we given up our pursuit of holy living too early?

I'm sure most men at some point get to the place where their thought process goes something like this: 'if I crucify the flesh, nail the attitudes, and I still can't beat it, then I may as well succumb to it. God knows I've tried. But I can't do it. I've got these urges—God needs to accept me as I am.' Let me be quite honest with you. There is a way out. There is a place of breakthrough. If you push past your disillusionment, you will arrive at a landscape of freedom.

Train your Mind

As we consider all of the above, we should not underestimate the depth of depravity in the human heart. The Bible is clear; the natural tendency and bias of the human heart towards sin is constant and strong.

'The human heart is the most deceitful of all things, and desperately wicked. Who really knows how bad it is?'

(Jeremiah 17:9—NLT)

In Galatians 5:19-21 Paul gives a list of 'the desires of the flesh.' He writes, 'the acts of the flesh are obvious: sexual immorality, impurity and debauchery; idolatry and witchcraft; hatred, discord, jealousy, fits of rage, selfish ambition, dissensions, factions and envy; drunkenness, orgies, and the like.' This list includes—among other things—a cross section of sexual misbehaviours and alternate lifestyle choices. I find it interesting that Paul specifies that these things originate from the flesh. They start as a natural internal pull from our own depraved hearts. They are not necessarily demonic or spiritual strongholds at this stage, but they begin in the destructive inclinations of our fallen, sinful nature.

When we follow the pull of the desires of the flesh and refuse to renew our minds, we make an intentional decision to board trains of thought that are en-route to perverse destinations. Dave Gilpin gives a helpful analogy that I will borrow here. Trains are regularly departing from platforms in our mind, and we have numerous opportunities to board these trains every day. When we make a decision to board a train, we can very easily lose track of time, staying on board for multiple stops. Eventually the train will lead us to the final destination—a city of habit.

These cities can be havens for unhealthy emotional ideas and ungodly lifestyles. When we move into one of these cities, the environment will always have a pervasive and destructive effect on our lives, ending up in strongholds.

The good news is that not only can we move out of these cities, but we can also make choices to board trains to alternate destinations. Other platforms harbour trains that will actually bring us back into the cities we were born to live in, places where great and positive habits are as natural to us as the unhealthy ones we embraced for so long.

Some of us have sex on the brain. Now is the perfect time to examine your hairpiece in more detail. What has been nesting in your mind? Is it wise to allow it to remain in residence? If you are harbouring some unwanted guests, don't panic! In some of the chapters that follow we will be discovering the best way to confront and deal with the things that have infiltrated our thinking.

Any thoughts on this chapter? Participate in the conversation on 🐦 twitter: @pfsbook #sexonthebrain or 📘 www.facebook.com/pfsbook

CHAPTER 10

THE MASS DEBATE

Is God okay with solo sex? Does he frown upon our choices to succumb to our physical appetites? Or does he understand that we just can't help it, honest? What is wrong with masturbation anyway?

As an ex-professional, I do have some opinion on the matter. There are in fact a number of problems with practising masturbation.

I'm not Hurting Anyone

I truly believe masturbation is a selfish act. Sex was designed by God to be enjoyed by a man and a woman in marriage, not by a man and his right hand in the bathroom. The Bible says that a man shall leave his father and mother and cleave to his wife. Nowhere does the Bible suggest that before or after leaving his father and mother a man should cleave to his penis. Though the Bible does say in Ecclesiastes, 'whatever a man's hand finds to do he should do it with all his might', I am reasonably confident that Solomon did not have masturbation in mind at this point. Ladies reading this paragraph, please excuse my crudeness. But take on board the challenge for yourself about the expression of lustful desires. Men and woman practising masturbation are carrying out a selfish act.

Some believers think that by masturbating they are not hurting anyone. 'I love Jesus,' they say. 'I even give money to charity. I help people in need—but I want to masturbate. I'm not hurting anyone.'

Unfortunately this is not true. You are hurting someone. Let's look at whom, exactly.

Harming Yourself

As with any sin, you are hurting yourself. You may not be inflicting pain upon yourself physically, but by serving yourself and your own appetites, you are doing spiritual damage that will affect your soul and your emotions. The solution to loneliness and heightened physical appetites was never meant to be porn and masturbation. The answer was always meant to be enjoyment of the intimate presence of God.

For many years, my justification for masturbation was scientific not theological. I based my behaviour on the fact that men have a biological need for the release of semen every twenty-four to seventy-two hours. I've read it somewhere in some scientific textbook. 'I am a man. I have regular strong desires for sexual release. This is my body at work. Who am I to argue with it? I have sexual needs, and when they arise, I will fulfil those needs by masturbation or any means necessary. It would actually be medically dangerous for me to avoid this fulfilment that my body demands'. Or so the argument goes.

Women could justify their sinful sexual fulfilment in a similar way. The sex drive of a woman can be justified by pointing to the fact that drives fluctuate with their hormonal cycle. Sometimes, for women too, the urge for relief becomes too strong to resist. 'I can't help it', you may say. 'As I near ovulation, I experience a stronger sexual desire.' Or maybe that desire is equally strong throughout the month and just too difficult to resist.

For men and women, these biological arguments become the angle we take in the justification for solo sexual expression. But let me ask you two questions.

What makes you think that you are bound by the desires of your physical body?

Is it possible that you are actually bound by something else?

I have found that, almost four years into complete abstinence, I have no problem maintaining my celibacy despite having spent eighteen years in which I regularly fulfilled my desires. As extreme as it may sound, celibacy is God's purpose for all of us while we are single, and celibacy is not just abstaining from sex.

Thou shalt not masturbate!

Masturbation and Fantasy

One of the most compelling arguments that masturbation is sinful has to do with the role of sexual fantasy.

Let's be honest with ourselves here.

Is it really possible to engage in masturbation without resorting to images that are clearly sinful? What about the teaching of Jesus in relation to lust at this point? In Matthew 5:27-30 (NIV) we read:

> *"You have heard that it was said, 'You shall not commit adultery.' But I tell you that anyone who looks at a woman lustfully has already committed adultery with her in his heart. If your right eye causes you to stumble, gouge it out and throw it away. It is better for you to lose one part of your body than for your whole body to be thrown into hell. And if your right hand causes you to stumble, cut it off and throw it away. It is better for you to lose one part of your body than for your whole body to go into hell."*

Now let's not carried away at this point over Jesus' use of figurative hyperbole here—his deliberate use of metaphor and exaggeration to make a point. If everyone who had a problem with masturbation took Jesus literally there would be a lot of one handed, blind people in the church. Let's be careful to respect what kind of language is being used here and why.

What's really important is that we appreciate Jesus' prohibition of lustful fantasies. The mind is a central facet of the human soul. Our imaginations are extremely powerful resources for good and ill. Jesus clearly teaches that it is not enough to refrain from committing the act of adultery (by which he means sex outside of marriage). We have to go further than that and reveal a righteousness that is internal not just external. In other words, we are called as Christians not just to refrain from sexual acts outside marriage. We are called not to fantasize in a way that is adulterous too.

In light of this, which of us can honestly say that it is possible to masturbate without engaging in fantasies that are immoral? While the Bible may be silent when it comes to the subject of masturbation, it certainly isn't silent when it comes to the subject of illicit sexual fantasies. These are regarded as adultery in the teaching of Jesus.

Perhaps this is where we can see the pernicious power of pornography. Today, at the click of a mouse, anyone can readily find themselves watching images that are the grossest expression of lustful fantasies. While not everyone who masturbates resorts to watching images on a screen, most resort to creating adulterous images in their minds. As soon as this happens a line has been crossed and people have certainly embraced more than 'a hint of sexual immorality' (Ephesians 5:3).

Theology and Biology

My genuine conviction is that your theology can conquer your biology here. If you deeply nurture your relationship with

Jesus, the priorities of your physical and spiritual demands will change with incredible ease.

We have long defended our rights to respond to our physical desires, but have we spent similar time responding to our spirit's call for intimacy with God? I honestly believe it is impossible to fulfil both of these desires simultaneously. Eventually something has got to give—either your relationship with God or your relationship with your hand.

I once heard somebody responding to questions about Jesus' celibacy by questioning whether he abstained from masturbation.

'Have you ever thought about Jesus performing other natural bodily functions?' he asked. 'Yet he still did them! You may not be able to picture Jesus on the toilet, far less him masturbating, but does this mean he didn't?'

Here's my response to that.

I can promise you, though Jesus did defecate, he definitely did not masturbate. His submission to the Holy Spirit meant that his desire was to do the Father's will and that meant abstaining from masturbation.

If by God's grace I can abstain from sexual expression from February 2010 up until now, Jesus was more than capable of abstaining for a lifetime. And he can help you to do the same while you remain unmarried. All you have to do is resolve to live a holy life, receive his empowering grace to do so, and nurture heartfelt intimacy with the Living God.

The Hyper-Grace Trap

When many Christians discuss their own sexual sin, they like to emphasise the grace of God. Of course they do! They want forgiveness and acceptance from God following any decision to rebel. After every fall they persuade themselves that God's grace has provided them with the pardon they have sought after.

The danger with this kind of reasoning is that grace can become something behind which we start to hide our sinful, dark behaviour. 'Have you been watching hardcore pornography and masturbating three times a day? Have you been fooling around with your girlfriend? Have you been having an afternoon of mutual masturbation or oral sex out of wedlock? Don't worry; the grace of God will cover you! He will forgive you.'

But is this really grace?

Or is this cheap grace—a cover up for our sins rather than the covering of our sin?

Cheap grace is not real grace.

Grace, as Dietrich Bonhoeffer said, is 'costly'.

Grace is the Power to Overcome

In much of our contemporary theology of grace, many of us have been severely short-changed. Grace is far more than acceptance and forgiveness of sinful people by God. Grace encompasses more than we could possibly imagine.

> *For the grace of God that bringeth salvation hath*
> *appeared to all men, teaching us that, denying*
> *ungodliness and worldly lusts, we should live soberly,*
> *righteously, and godly, in this present world*

(Titus 2:11-12—ERV)

English translations sometimes do not do justice to the colour and emphasis of some of the original language of the Bible. The word 'grace' in the passage above is described as something that teaches us *how to live*. What does grace mean then? *Strong's Concordance* defines grace as 'the divine influence upon the heart, and its reflection in the life'. Grace is empowering! Its presence affects the lives we live out on a daily basis.

Grace is not something that covers up our sexually immoral acts. Grace is what empowers us to overcome sin when we choose to obey God's Word.

The Bible sets a standard, and that standard includes sexual purity. God gives us grace, which means he literally empowers us to fulfil the requirements and expectations that seem so impossible to keep. By God's grace, we not only receive Jesus' forgiveness when we sin, we actually receive the divine ability to not practice it.

Remember, according to the Bible we are partakers of 'the divine nature'. I am not saying that we will *never* sin, but the power has been put in our hands to achieve holiness. We still have a choice to sin or not to sin. But when we have access to the divine nature, we can realistically expect to achieve a life of premarital celibacy and abstinence.

For many living outside of this level of grace, it would seem that what is actually required is an impossible amount of effort and self-discipline. To the average human trying to live out his Christianity, it feels exhausting. Could it be that this is because you have not cashed in fully on the free gift of God's grace? If you do, it will help you achieve what truth demands of you.

Grace is not a certificate of indulgence giving us the license to watch pornography or continue daily sexual fulfilment outside of marriage, with no consequences or repercussions. Grace has far further reaching implications than this. Grace is about effortless freedom. I really believe it that this is not just pie in the sky when you die. It's enjoyable today.

So submit your sexuality to the rule of God, including the issue of masturbation. There really shouldn't be a mass debate here. As Paul wrote in 1 Thessalonians 4:3-8 (NIV):

It is God's will that you should be sanctified: that you should avoid sexual immorality; that each of you should learn to control your own body in a way that is holy and honourable, not in passionate lust like the pagans, who do not know God; and that in this matter no one should wrong or take advantage of a brother or sister. The Lord will punish all those who commit such sins, as we told you and warned you before. For God did not call us to be impure, but to live a holy life. Therefore, anyone who rejects this instruction does not reject a human being but God, the very God who gives you his Holy Spirit.

Any thoughts on this chapter? Participate in the conversation on twitter: @pfsbook #themassdebate or www.facebook.com/pfsbook

CHAPTER 11

GROPING IN THE DARK

Whether you are on your own or with someone, it seems that physical darkness intensifies the process of temptation. It is so often when the lights are out that 'cheeky' antics start suggesting themselves to our imaginations, especially when we are in bed. The word 'cheeky' is, of course, extremely inappropriate when describing sexually sinful acts. It makes light of something that is actually spiritually dangerous. Our culture regards such acts as 'cheeky.' The Bible regards them as destructive.

Some of you may share the 'cheeky' view which says that a little fumble in the dark is harmless enough. After all, isn't groping in the dark between two consenting adults? What's the problem?

This is a view I once shared but which I never publicly acknowledged. It was a convenient justification for my own sinful actions in private. After all I've experienced and studied, I can never affirm this view again.

The Poison of Secrecy

The spiritual world is divided into two kingdoms: the kingdom of light and the kingdom of darkness. The kingdom of light is God's kingdom. The kingdom of darkness is the devil's kingdom. Both of these kingdoms fall into the 'unseen realm';

we can't see them with our physical eyes. If our spiritual eyes are closed then we will be unable to see either God's kingdom or the devil's.' Groping in the dark' is our default setting.

In Acts 26:17-18 Jesus says to Paul, 'I am sending you to open their eyes so that they may turn from darkness into light and from the dominion of Satan to God...'

Here Jesus highlights to Paul the truth and reality of darkness and light. God appoints and commissions Paul as a messenger to the world and this mandate relates specifically to 'opening the eyes' of those in darkness. The eyes of the world were closed, leaving them in darkness. As devout as he was in his pursuit of the religious life of Judaism, Paul's eyes were closed to the fact that Christ was the Jewish Messiah until he had a rude awakening on the road to Damascus. This encounter with the living Christ initially affected his physical eyes but it also led him to make some seismic adjustments to his spiritual understanding. Our eyes are also shut too. Many of us are oblivious to the darkness that surrounds us.

There are many characteristics of the kingdom of darkness to which we are blind but one of the most important and the most destructive can be summed up in the word 'secrecy.' Groping in the dark is something we do in secret. While this habit or act remains a secret, it will always maintain a strong hold over us. Bring it to the light, however, and it starts to lose its power. Its grip over our lives begins to be loosed. This is why the Apostle John wrote:

> *This is the message we have heard from him and proclaim to you, that God is light, and in him is no darkness at all. If we say we have fellowship with him while we walk in darkness, we lie and do not practice the truth. But if we walk in the light, as he is in the light, we have fellowship with one another, and the blood of Jesus his Son cleanses us from all sin.*
>
> (1 John 1:5-7, ESV)

It is also why Paul says in Ephesians 5:11-14:

Take no part in the unfruitful works of darkness, but instead expose them. For it is shameful even to speak of the things that they do in secret. But when anything is exposed by the light, it becomes visible, for anything that becomes visible is light. Therefore it says,

"Awake, O sleeper,
and arise from the dead,
and Christ will shine on you."

Accountability is the Antidote

If we are engaged in something of a sensitive and toxic nature, it can be very difficult to find the courage to share our struggle with someone else, especially a Christian. This often means that we *never* share our struggle with anyone. The strength of sin is in its secrecy, and as long as we keep sin buried, it continues to have power. When we bravely bring it out into the open, addictions begin a process of dilution and their hold over us decreases.

From this we can see how important it is to have other people in our lives with whom we can share our struggles, ask for prayer, and find our freedom. While bondages are developed in isolation, they are broken in community. Accountability is therefore a vital, albeit painful, discipline that will benefit us all. It is an essential prerequisite for our healing and our freedom. As the Apostle James wrote, 'confess your sins to one another and pray for one another that you may be healed' (James 5:16-17, ESV).

Perhaps at this point it would be helpful to return to my own testimony, and especially the importance of confessing my secret struggles.

Before my point of breakthrough when God set me free, I had been praying with my parents for fifteen minutes a day. In

February, after about eight weeks of doing this, I was set free. Interestingly, after we had been praying for about two weeks, God revealed to me that I needed to do something about my secrecy issues. He challenged me to open up to my dad and ask him to pray about my sexual struggles. God told me that my secrecy wasn't helping my progress. Accountability was something that I had neglected for quite a long time.

Once again we see the dangers of keeping our struggles hidden and the importance of cultivating transparency and honesty with others. As John the Apostle wrote:

> And this is the judgment: the light has come into the world, and people loved the darkness rather than the light because their works were evil. For everyone who does wicked things hates the light and does not come to the light, lest his works should be exposed. But whoever does what is true comes to the light, so that it may be clearly seen that his works have been carried out in God

(John 3:19-21, ESV)

God's Revealing Light

The guilt and shame associated with sin and its addictive nature can cause us to find solace in secrecy. This eventually becomes a burden too heavy to bear. Rather than live in darkness and secrecy, our true freedom is found in light and truth. That is why we should pray using the words of King David, who knew a thing or two about bringing secret sin into the light:

> Send out your light and your truth; let them lead me;
> let them bring me to your holy hill

(Psalm 43:3, ESV)

Staying in secrecy means that I have lied to myself in an attempt at self-preservation. I'm trying to Photoshop my public image, consequently distorting others' opinions of me to make myself look better than I actually am. The truth is, when people get close enough to see who we really are, our attempts to manipulate our image are all in vain.

While it is possible for shadows to attack us even when we are in the light, it is when we are in the darkness that they have real power to hurt us. That being the case, we need to put secrecy to death and allow our hidden addictions to be dispersed by the light. Only then do they lose their power.

We can deny the severity of our sin and refuse to acknowledge and confront it, but this stops the light from exposing our darkness. We may successfully 'protect' ourselves from the light—and the embarrassment that it might cause us for a while—but by continuing to grope in the dark, we minimise the possibility of our finding a solution. Not only that, but we fool ourselves if we think that these things will remain hidden forever. They will not. As King David wrote, 'our iniquities, our secret heart and its sins [which we would so like to conceal even from ourselves], you have set in the [revealing] light of your countenance' (Psalm 90:8, AMP).

We tend to conceal our sin even from ourselves, let alone from other people. But the One person we cannot hide sin from—even if we want to—is God. God highlights our secrecy in 'the revealing light of his countenance'. His light floods every dark crevice of our hidden life. When you have been in the dark for a long time, the dazzling light of the presence of God will be difficult to adjust to. We all initially have to squint in order to regain a level of clarity.

Faithful Wounds

The etymology of the word, 'vulnerability', is very interesting. It comes from the Latin word *vulnus* which means 'wound'.

Everyone who desires to grow spiritually needs to put themselves in a place of accountability, a place where we allow someone else to challenge us. These challenges can feel like a wounding but the Bible says 'faithful are the wounds of a friend' (Proverbs 27.6). In other words, when a friend challenges us about some secret, destructive habit, that challenge is a sign to us that they are a faithful friend. True friends won't allow us to stay imprisoned. True friends tell us that we are prisoners and help us to break out of our chains.

We all need friends who are prepared to wound us faithfully. We all need accountability-partners who are not afraid to 'wound' us with words of truth expressed with grace. Having such people around us is absolutely vital if we are to be set free from sexual bondages. No one can effectively come into the light and dispel their darkness without other trusted people holding their hands and leading them out of their pit of destruction and despair. We need each other.

So don't resist the challenge to cultivate accountability, and don't take offence when those you are submitted to in love tell you things you don't want to hear. It's always easier to find people who will agree with us and collude with our compromise. It's much harder, nobler and more heroic to surround yourself with those who will tell you what you don't want to hear, and in the process turn your compromise into commitment. Yes, the wounds of a friend may hurt for a moment. But the fruit from those wounds will last a lifetime.

Letting friends shine their torch into one of our dark places costs us something. Our Gollum-like eyes have become accustomed to shadows and darkness. Believe me having experienced the difficulty of being completely transparent about the depth of my own depravity, I know what I'm talking about. Light hurts!

Intentional vulnerability, with key people who we know will ask us difficult questions, is a very healthy part of getting free and keeping our lives in the light of God's truth. You cannot experience sexual healing without the wounds of a friend or two.

The Spirit of Truth

One of the titles for the Holy Spirit in the Bible is 'the spirit of truth'. Truth is one of God's primary attributes. He cannot and will not lie. Truth is at the very core of his divine nature. Spend time in God's presence and you spend time in the presence of truth. If we are living lives of deception, this will cause tension. Spending time with God will either cause us to be vulnerable and open to transformation or it will make us run away from him and hide, like Adam and Eve in the Garden.

Have you hidden sinful things? Have you buried them deep in a place of secrecy for so long that that they are now rotting inside of you and making you sick? By repeated decisions to remain in darkness, you will cultivate an environment where you drink from dirty, stagnant water not from pure, living water. You need to acknowledge truthfully where you really are before God. You need to let the Spirit of Truth have access to every part of your life. You need to proclaim, 'no more groping in the dark, no more cheeky antics in the bedroom, it's time to live and walk in the light.'

The kingdom of darkness is a very real kingdom. It's not a fictional realm from the *Star Wars* universe. We are not talking about some mythical 'dark side'; we are talking about a very real devil and his very real shadows. They have a destructive and toxic agenda—to keep as many as possible outside of the kingdom of light, and to immobilise those who are in the light by tempting them to 'grope in the dark.'

This kingdom of light and the kingdom of darkness are in direct opposition. They cannot coexist or cohabit. In the unseen realm there are spiritual battles going on all the time—battles which affect us but about which we are often unaware. When we come into the light our eyes become open to this reality and our other spiritual senses are tuned into the unseen world. We come into the revelation that the spiritual world is very real and that a grope in the dark is not just a physical act; it is opening a door to spiritual darkness too.

To understand all this, we need to let the Spirit of Truth have free reign in every nook and cranny of our soul.

No door must be closed to him.

He must be allowed to shine his light everywhere.

And we must let him do that.

Any thoughts on this chapter? Participate in the conversation on 🐦 twitter: @pfsbook #gropinginthedark or 📘 www.facebook.com/pfsbook

CHAPTER 12

TEAM PORN

Everyone knows about the Ten Commandments—the rules for holy living given by God to Moses in the Old Testament—that we are *supposed* to observe. When people think about sin, they think about the breaking of these rules and commandments. For many, the notion of sin is really just about the breaking of a law or a commandment. Wrong! Though this is a part of it, it's not the full picture.

Sin is actually about picking sides or picking teams. When you choose to sin or not to sin, you align yourself with one of two teams. There is God's team or the devil's team; there is no grey area. Whenever you sin sexually, you make a decision to be a part of a team. You align yourself with it and side against the opposition. Whether you like it or not, in your decision making in the area of sexuality, you are picking teams.

When you practice sexual sin, you take a home shirt for Team Porn and put it on. Maybe nobody knows about your struggles and sinful choices. In the day-to-day life you live this could be the case. Family, friends, spouse and church leadership may be completely unaware of what you're doing. But the sobering reality is that in the spiritual realm every angel and demon within range can see that you are on Team Porn. You can't put on a mask or a false front. Apart from your Team Porn T-shirt, you are standing in your birthday suit. Jesus and the hosts of heaven can see what shirt you've

111

put on, what team you've chosen. As the Risen Jesus says in Revelation 16:15:

'Look, I come like a thief! Blessed is the one who stays awake and remains clothed, so as not to go naked and be shamefully exposed.'

Jesus tells us that it is very much to our advantage that we remain prepared for his return and that involves wearing appropriate spiritual clothes and making sure that we're not naked. Nakedness involves exposing ourselves, causing ourselves great shame. It means that we live a double life. By day, we are a smartly dressed respectable employee and an exemplary example. By night, it's a different story, and we literally let it all hang out.

Spiritual nakedness means that we are not what people think we are. As a result of this, our effectiveness is hindered. Because of our sin, we put limitations on what God can do through our lives. He still loves us, but he hates our sin. He watches in sorrow as our porn habit drags us into lukewarm living, and lukewarm living leads to a very unpleasant conclusion.

'So, because you are lukewarm, and neither hot nor cold, I will spit you out of my mouth'

(Revelation 3:16, ESV)

The Devil's Team Tactics

I believe that living in a compromising way by sinning sexually sends clear messages not only to God but also to the devil. But how exactly does Satan pick up on what we're doing? And is it not a little antiquated to think he could attach himself to our secret addictions?

I think that the devil and his team operate like sharks. Sharks have an acute sense of smell. Even a drop of blood in the ocean can be detected far away. After picking up the scent, they move in its direction and find the source. Once this has happened, you have to pity the wounded creature on the other end of the scent trail.

When we begin to succumb to the temptation to sin sexually, we effectively cut ourselves and release a flow of blood into a shark-infested sea. The enemy is attracted to pornography like a shark to blood. He becomes excited when he picks up the scent of premarital or extra-marital sex and makes every effort to attach himself to it. Even when we skirt around the edges, spending time reliving memories that were once exciting to us, this thinking is enough to attract the kingdom of darkness and start a feeding frenzy. Before we know it, we have turned ourselves into shark bait. Eventually we will be completely shredded.

Because this feeding frenzy is happening in the spiritual realm, we are likely to be unaware of it with our natural senses. Instead, for a moment we actually enjoy what's going on. The physical aspect of what we are doing has immediate benefits, but the spiritual side is a different story. Our spiritual senses are often numbed, and if this is the case, we cannot expect to be aware of or remain protected from the onslaught we have invited.

Blood Coated Popsicles

I remember once hearing an illustration that has subsequently been widely used. It has to do with the process by which Eskimo hunters catch wolves.

The Inuit people apparently take a razor-sharp knife and cover the blade with a layer of fresh blood from a dead seal. Within a matter of minutes of applying this blood, it freezes solid to the blade. The hunters then paint a second coat of blood over the same blade. This again freezes very quickly. This process is repeated several more times until the knife resembles a blood-red popsicle.

The Eskimo hunters then plunge the hilt of the knife into the snow and wait. The scent of the blood does not take long to attract a hungry wolf. The wolf wastes no time in refreshing himself with the blood-coated iced lolly. Soon the wolf has actually licked off the surface blood. But in the process, the wolf's tongue becomes completely numb due to the freezing temperature of the blade.

The wolf continues to lick the blade, and in so doing slashes his tongue to pieces. The unfortunate animal is oblivious to the pain due to his numbed tongue. Now unknowingly tasting his own blood, the wolf continues to indulge until he lies unconscious and drained of life. The wolf remains in a heap on the snow until the Eskimo hunter returns to collect his prize.

Like me, you may have caught the scent of a Popsicle and been overcome with an overwhelming appetite. You too have been oblivious to the destructive spiritual nature of sexual sin. You were driven by the intense strength of your physical appetites, and your pursuit of sexual fulfilment drained your spirit of the source of true spiritual life. You didn't realise that this steak lolly served rare was set as a trap for your destruction. Someone has been preventing you from living your life to the full for years. You never realised that because your sin had caused you to become blind, your addictions had led you to the place where you couldn't think clearly any more. As the Bible puts it, 'the natural person does not accept the things of the Spirit of God, for they are folly to him, and he is not able to understand them because they are spiritually discerned' (1 Corinthians 2:14, ESV).

But it's not too late. You can leave Team Porn.

Choose Christ's Team

When it comes to sexual temptation, it can often be almost overpoweringly alluring. This is because it entices us in the area of our deepest longings and strongest appetites. When it comes to us it comes in a passionate and impulsive form. It is hard to resist. But we must resist. Choosing to yield to temptation is choosing to yield to the wrong team. It is a decision to ally oneself with team Porn. Choosing to resist is a decision to side oneself with God's team. Siding with God's team is a decision that we need to make not just for a single moment but for a lifetime.

Joshua made a lifetime decision for his entire family when it came to the issue of 'allegiance'. In no uncertain terms, he told everyone within earshot what team he would support and where his allegiance lay.

> 'Choose this day whom you will serve … as for me and my house we will serve the Lord.'

> (Joshua 24:15, ESV)

Joshua had made his decision, and he would stick with it, but it was not a decision Joshua could make for those around him. They would each need to decide for themselves about their allegiance. 'Choose this day whom you will serve,' Joshua cried. In other words, 'pick which team you will align yourself with and stick with that team!'

Today, for some people, reading this is a wake-up call. It's decision time. Are you going to continue to align yourself with the devil? Are you going to let him manage and dictate your life, your decisions, and your tactics? Are you going to allow shadows to be your team mates? Are you going to play a destructive game for the rest of your life?

Playing for the devil's team has devastating consequences. Here are a few:

We make a conscious choice to live independently from God in our sexuality. We separate ourselves from him.

Because we are living by the impetus of 'the flesh', our actions and choices are dictated by physical desires.

We progressively disassociate ourselves from the spiritual source that would help us to deal with life's stresses and temptations.

Our mind is constantly filled with and influenced by wrong thoughts and images.

Our emotions are continuously affected by destructive impulses, bringing us deeper down into the pit of despair and depression.

If we join the devil's team we will start to take on board the culture of our team. The voices of fellow players will echo the sentiments of our own hearts, reinforcing and validating tragic choices and toxic habits.

However, if we open ourselves up to God and join or rejoin his team, we start to have a bias towards the culture of Jesus. We become aligned with integrity. Uncompromising discipleship becomes our team objective.

The devil keeps our subscription to Team Porn active by feeding us with deceit. Some of the propaganda sent our way can sound something like this:

This habit, mindset or emotion I am dealing with is simply a part of who I am.

Freedom might be realistic for other people, but my case is different, and it could never work for me.

I could never have a relationship with God like that person has.

Jesus could never use me.

The truth is there is no shame in admitting that you are wearing the wrong shirt. You can align with another team, particularly when the captain of that team is Jesus Christ. If you come to him, he has promised he will never reject you. However worthless and ashamed you may feel, he wants you in his team and he has a special position and role for you.

He has the power to remove your old shirt, transform your life, give you new skills, and put a winning mentality in your heart. You don't have to wallow around in the mud any more like a loser. You can climb the steps and receive your medal of victory.

Join Jesus' team today.

You'll be more than a champion if you do.

Any thoughts on this chapter? Participate in the conversation on ▼ twitter: @pfsbook #teamporn or ▪ www.facebook.com/pfsbook

CHAPTER 13

THREE IN A BED

As an unmarried and single man I sleep alone but snuggling up in the warmth of my duvet, I have company. I may be unaware of their presence but two friends are with me.

God says in the Book of Genesis that he created us in his image. This 'image' refers to the divine blueprint according to which all of us are made. We all share the same key features because we are all of us composed to reflect God's being. So what does that actually mean?

Have you ever seen a set of matryoshka dolls? They are the hollow wooden Russian dolls that contain smaller dolls positioned inside one another.

Imagine three dolls, one inside each other, fitting perfectly. Outwardly there appears to be only one doll, but in reality there are three.

The Bible teaches that we are actually made of three things, even though it might appear outwardly that we are only composed of one.

Outwardly it might seem that we are just physical beings, living human bodies. But inside our bodies there are two other vital aspects to us—our souls and spirits.

What this means is that a human person is one being but three parts. This tripartite being is composed of our bodies, souls and spirits.

And the reason why we are three-in-one like this is because we are created in the image of God, and he himself is one being but three persons—Father, Son and Holy Spirit.

Spirit, Soul, Body

Created in the image of the Triune God, we are all of us composed of three things—body, soul and spirit. But unlike God's triune state, our tripartite nature is not always in harmonious agreement. Often each part of us is eager for dominance. In other words your body, soul and spirit each have their own opinion, and they won't always agree about what you should do.

For most people, the biggest and best maintained of the three distinct parts of their nature is their body. The 'body' is well exercised and nurtured. This is not only in regard to physical exercise but also in relation to physical appetites. Whether it's sleep, food, drink, or other pleasures, the body has not been denied what it wants. For many, the body is in the seat of power. Their body is in charge, to the detriment of the rest of their being.

What about the soul? Our soul encompasses our emotions, our mind and intellect and our will. Our soul is where we feel happiness, joy and love. We can equally feel anger, hatred and resentment. It is also the filter for logic and reasoned decision-making. Our soul contains the developing shape of our personality. For many people, soulful emotions are actually on the throne of their lives. I know that, for me, this was the case for a long time.

This leaves only one aspect, the human spirit. To be honest, for a long time I struggled to understand exactly what my spirit was, but now I think I get it! Our spirit is our God-consciousness. In basic terms, it's the part of me that was designed to connect to my creator.

The Bible teaches that God desires to communicate with me, and he uses my spirit as the receiver. If I rarely or never attempt to tune in to him, then my screen will display nothing but fuzz. As I seek to connect to him, he seeks to connect to me. I start to receive the transmission. It's faint at first, but as I spend more time investing in my relationship with Jesus, I find that a greater level of clarity comes.

The human spirit is therefore that part of us that connects with God spiritually. It is that part of us which comes alive when we make the choice to follow Jesus and the life of the Spirit floods our being. It is the most important part of our being. Far from being in the back seat, it should be in the driver's seat. Our spirit should actually be at the forefront of our decision-making, over and above our soul and body.

The Control Centre

An internal cry comes from every area of our tripartite nature, each demanding to be heard. All three parts fight for the platform of control. Normally body and soul receive the greatest attention because they are the loudest. The voice of our spirit is potentially the most significant but for many it is the least audible because it is the part of us that has received the least attention. For this reason, it often has pitiful levels of influence. Whatever sounds our spirit makes, they are drowned out by the noisier, more demanding siblings, 'body' and 'soul'. If we exercised our spirits more, we would start to change the dynamics of power in our tripartite nature. We would begin to pay more attention to the still small voice of our spirit rather than always responding to the deafening and demanding 'toddler tantrums' of our bodies and the insistent cries of our soul—our emotions and intellect.

I once read a book by an American preacher called Kenneth Hagin. He put it like this: 'I am a Spirit, I have a Soul, and I live in a Body'. I like this because I believe it accurately identifies God's original intention for the pecking order of our human life. Our spirit is supposed to be in charge and our soul (mind, emotions and will) and bodily appetites should be submitted to our spirit.

We need to learn to live a life of submission. What does this mean? And what does it look like?

Firstly, our spirit should be submitted to God. It should be strong and healthy, regularly built up through spiritual disciplines and a healthy spiritual diet.

Secondly, there is our soul. Submission or rebellion in the soul-part of our lives has the capacity to build up our spirit or damage it. By appropriately feeding the soul with godly thoughts and emotions, we can deepen our intimacy with God at the level of our spirits.

Thirdly, our physical bodies should be submitted to God. If we don't submit our physical bodies to God, the inevitable response is that our physical appetites will have damaging effects on our spirit, causing it to become dulled and desensitised.

If we are to live lives as God intended—which is life in all its fullness—then our spirit needs to be filled with the Holy Spirit. Once the human spirit is submitted to the Holy Spirit, the soul can then begin to think with a renewed mind and heart. Then the appetites of our bodies can respond to the voice of the resurrected spirit and the inclinations of our renewed soul by behaving in a Christ-like way.

True Freedom

This is all the more important for us as the return of Christ draws nearer and nearer and it is why Paul was led to pray for one of his church congregations with reference to their tripartite nature:

'I pray God your whole spirit and soul and body be preserved blameless unto the coming of our Lord Jesus Christ.'

(1 Thessalonians 5:23, KJB)

This verse more than any other shows how important it is to have our spirit, soul and body completely submitted to God. Starting with my spirit (the first thing Paul mentions), then my soul, then my body—every part of me—needs to be maintained in a constant state of wholeness and holiness until Christ returns on the last day.

We must be so careful not to create a fractured trinity in which the spirit—the God-conscious part of our being— becomes fragmented and separated, no longer performing its God-ordained role of influencing all that we think, say and do.

The body and its appetites cannot be allowed to become the control centre of our lives.

Let's keep our spirits filled with the Spirit of Jesus.

Let's keep our souls—our emotions, intellect, imagination, choices—obedient to our Christ-centred spirits.

Let's keep our bodies, with all their appetites, under the influence of human souls and spirits which are living in alignment with the Holy Spirit.

Let me encourage you to think about your own life in the light of your spirit, soul and body. Give it some consideration. Where is the seat of power in your life? Is it your emotions, your intellect? Or could it be that your physical body and its appetites are driving you?

As you allow the Holy Spirit to testify to your spirit that you are a royally adopted child of God (Romans 8:16), you will be led more and more by the Holy Spirit (Romans 8:14) and grow more and more to enjoy the glorious freedom of the children of God (Romans 8:21)—a freedom in which your soul is flooded with the love and joy of the Father (Romans 8:15) and your bodily desires are submitted to the Holy Spirit (Romans 8:10-13).

This is a life free from sexual addictions.

It is wholeness and health as God intended.

It is true freedom.

Any thoughts on this chapter? Participate in the conversation on ✐ twitter: @pfsbook #threeinabed or f www.facebook.com/pfsbook

CHAPTER 14

WRESTLING PERSONAL DEMONS

Have you ever seen the movie *Nacho Libre*? Actor Jack Black plays an aspiring wrestler who finds a tag team partner to accompany him in his quest for glory. Neither man looks like conventional wrestling material. If you saw me, you would agree that I would be an equally ridiculous choice for a career in wrestling. I've always been a lanky and gangly sort of bloke, and even though I'm slim, I've got a pot belly which is abnormally disproportionate to the rest of me. I think I'll steer clear of wrestling rings!

Don't worry. This chapter is not focusing on my unfulfilled career in wrestling. It's actually about one of the key realisations I came to in my victory over sexual sin and emotional turmoil. This is the realisation that we are participating in spiritual warfare, a wrestling match with an extremely evil opponent.

It's Not Cricket

Spiritual warfare is not something that people want to talk about. From my experience, it seems to be a subject that is seldom mentioned in any depth or detail in most churches today. In some churches it's viewed as a weird and ethereal topic. Why, I have to wonder, is it being sidestepped and avoided? When I've asked this question it seems that the general consensus is that it's because it's not regarded as a seeker sensitive subject. On one level, I can understand this argument. You don't want to freak seekers out by becoming top heavy on your discussion about Satan and demons. However, there must be a place *somewhere* to address this issue otherwise people will think they're joining a luxury cruise ship when in fact the church is much more like a warship.

But it's not just that this topic is neglected. It is also commonly misunderstood.

A frequently held misconception about spiritual warfare goes something like this: 'if I leave Satan and demons alone, Satan and demons will leave me alone'. If only this were the case. Having read this far in my book you should realise that this is false. My story—and more importantly the testimony of Scripture—bears out how shadows are constantly at work seeking to undermine and destroy the lives of Christians and non-Christians alike.

We mustn't therefore either neglect spiritual warfare or misunderstand it.

Nor—I should add—must we minimise it.

Depending on where you're from, you may or may not be familiar with the sport of cricket. Originating on the playing fields of England, cricket has traditionally always been regarded as a civilised sport. In the longer form of the game there is a break for lunch. Both teams sit down after the first part of the day to enjoy cucumber sandwiches and scones with cream and conserve. They have a tea break mid afternoon. Both teams often join each other for drinks afterwards.

In spiritual conflict there are no cucumber sandwiches on the menu. There is no halftime, no tea break, and no cavorting and revelling afterwards.

Spiritual warfare is not comedic wrestling either.

The world is not a demilitarised zone. A spiritual war rages day and night and in this war the devil's tactics are plain nasty. He and his demons fight dirty.

Spiritual Wrestling

Let's take a moment to read one of the classic passages in the Bible when it comes to spiritual warfare.

Finally, be strong in the Lord and in his mighty power. Put on the full armour of God so that you can take your stand against the devil's schemes. For our struggle (or wrestling match) is not against flesh and blood, but against the rulers, against the authorities, against the powers of this dark world and against the spiritual forces of evil in the heavenly realms. Therefore put on the full armour of God, so that when the day of evil comes, you may be able to stand your ground, and after you have done everything, to stand.'

(Ephesians 6:10-13, NIV)

The King James Version of the Bible actually starts this passage in Ephesians 6 with the words, 'for we wrestle not'. That just about says it. This is true for a majority of Christians. Called to fight against the enemy, they wrestle not! They remain completely uninvolved in the battle against the devil's schemes.

Wrestling is actually a very helpful analogy for understanding the type of battle we are in. We may not wear exotic accessories and colourful leotards, but we do climb into a wrestling ring every day to do battle with a dangerous opponent. And this fight is not staged, it is real.

Most of us are actually ignorant of the extent or even existence of this battle. This means that we live under the domination and control of the devil without us realising it. We're in a half-nelson and we don't even know it.

The devil climbs into the ring intent on our destruction. Even if we are not focused on the fight, he is very much alert to it and ready to take advantage of our every weakness. For most people, thinking about pornography, masturbation or an intimate moment with another person as a spiritual wrestling match is completely outside of their framework. The same could be said of emotional issues like depression or anger. We believe that these emotional problems are intrinsic to us—a part of our makeup, our personality. We believe the lie that lust, anger, despair and depression are purely human responses to the external pressures we face. Not so! The thoughts and feelings that are being sown into our souls by the enemy are not being recognised for what they actually are. This makes the devil's job a very easy one.

For much of my life, I had lost the wrestling match for sexual purity before I'd even begun. If I'm honest, for a number of years I was of the opinion that it made more sense to succumb to sinful behaviour than to resist it and wrestle against it. Historically, I already knew the outcome of my resistance to the drives I had. It would save a lot of time and energy if I just skipped to the end step (succumbing to my sexual urges or depression) with no resistance. There were times where I spent hours unable to sleep in my attempts to resist the urge to masturbate, only eventually to bow to the pressure to do it. Was it really worth the excruciating effort?

The answer is an emphatic yes. Which would you prefer, to be pinned down by the enemy or to pin him down? Your responsibility is not to lie down, roll over and give in. Your role is to stand, resist, fight and overcome. You were never called to be a victim. You were called to be a victor—to be more than a conqueror in the spiritual fight.

Our job in this wrestling match with the kingdom of darkness is to pin down our enemy. In the rules of wrestling, a particular battle has been won or lost once either wrestler has been pinned down. The devil is trying to pin us down, but if we resist him, we can actually come into a place of triumph by decisively pinning him down.

The truth is we don't just fight once. We fight continuously. These wrestling matches will continue throughout our lives and we have little or no warning as to when the next one will be. Just because the trend of recent years or months suggests the enemy has been having the upper hand, this does not mean that it will continue to be this way. He may have won a recent battle, but today is a new day, and God's mercies are new as well.

Suspending our Disbelief

'Come on David.' I hear you say, 'Do you really believe that? These things you're talking about—such as lust and depression—are heightened subjective emotions not evidence of demonic attack. Aren't you attributing purely human, psychological experiences to supernatural causes? Haven't we evolved beyond this kind of mythical thinking?'

In his classic book on spiritual conflict, *The Screwtape Letters*, C.S. Lewis said something which has been quoted often. We would be wise to remember it. He wrote, 'there are two equal and opposite errors into which our race can fall about the devils (demons). One is to disbelieve in their existence. The other is to believe, and to feel an excessive and unhealthy interest in them. They themselves are equally pleased with both errors and hail a materialist or a magician with the same delight'.

When it comes to spiritual warfare, there are generally two traps that Christians fall into:

People who disproportionately focus on the devil and demons as the sole cause of every problem.

People who disproportionately focus on 'the flesh' as the reason for their issues.

There are massive problems with both extremes. You have people in both groups who overemphasise either the devil or the flesh and neglect the part played by the other. Both groups are taking an unbalanced stance in their theology. This results in their long-term captivity.

There are people who are not living in victory because they have turned up to fight at the wrong ring entirely. Some people are trying to fight the devil when they should be 'crucifying their flesh'. Others have been attempting to 'crucify the flesh' for years, but they have been punching at thin air.

Paul once described himself like this: 'I do not fight like a man beating the air' (1 Corinthians 9:26). He understood that a man 'beating the air' is doing nothing except wearing himself out. When we stand in the correct ring and carefully engage our opponent, we are not punching the air. Our punches are effective, they will hurt the enemy, and we will win. But if we throw our punches in the wrong ring, we will lose energy and heart concurrently.

We need to master the conflicts in both rings—the ring of the flesh and the ring of the enemy. Don't be deceived, we can nail our fleshly attitudes. If this weren't the case, Paul would have never told us to crucify the flesh. In addition, we can pin down the devil. You can and you will take him out.

Exercising Discernment

Because there are different forces at work, we do need discernment to distinguish whether something is an issue of the flesh or of the devil. God helps us to make this distinction as we continue to nurture our relationship with Jesus. The closer you are to Jesus, the greater your discernment will be.

When you're in a fight and your opponent knows your Achilles Heel, he will aim for it. He will make sure he capitalises on that weak spot every time he can. In my case, the enemy had been watching me for years. He knew exactly how to push me to the 'nth' degree. The same is true for you too. The devil has found the pressure points that can immobilise you if you let him. He knows what buttons to push in order to bring you down and pin you down, causing you to succumb to his pressure and become a slave to your temptations.

But you don't need to be defeated. You are not called to be a casualty of war. You are actually a well equipped active member of God's army—the army that wins! You may have deserted from the front line for a season but God is your commanding officer and he's calling you to return to duty.

For you to do this effectively you must understand that you're wrestling against three things. This is not something you should be overly concerned about. You have three allies fighting with you—the Father, the Son and the Holy Spirit. And these three persons of the undivided Trinity are far more powerful than your three opponents.

So what are the three enemies we fight against?

They are what the Bible calls the world, the flesh and the devil.

World

The world (*kosmos* in the New Testament Greek) refers to the systems, structures and ideologies of the culture in which you live and which have an influence over your beliefs and behaviour. These systems, structures and ideologies are hostile to God because they are governed by principalities and powers—by evil forces in the spiritual realm—which hate everything to do with the God of the Bible. They are profoundly anti-Christian and their intention is to create cultures in which Christianity will not survive and in which Christians will either renounce their faith or compromise. The world is therefore not an easy place for a Christian to live. Its hatred of Jesus is something which we are warned about frequently in the Bible. The world wants you to believe what it believes and behave in the way that it behaves. It promotes deception at every turn and as a Christian you are called to wrestle with its lies and conquer through your commitment to the truth of the Word of God.

Flesh

'The flesh' is a term used by the apostle Paul to refer to the innate human bias towards sin. The flesh is the 'body' part of the 'spirit, soul, body' trinity. It is also called the 'sinful nature'. The flesh is therefore one of our enemies. We have a natural inclination towards sin. We have to live in this fallen, anti-Christian world with a constant, internal predisposition toward rebellion. This rebellion can manifest itself in any number of ways, including pride of life, the craving for possessions, and especially the unrestrained and sinful expression of sexual passions. The flesh is a potent enemy in the wrestling matches which we have to fight on a continuous basis as Christians.

Devil

As far as the Bible is concerned, the devil exists. It's as simple as that. He is known by many names—'the evil one,' 'the devil,' 'Satan,' 'the father of lies,' the destroyer,' to name just a few. He is the organizing, malevolent intelligence behind the spiritual and moral darkness which we see in the world today. This darkness is not the product of purely human choices or merely sociological factors. While we should not give the devil any undue attention, the fact is he is real and he is the orchestrator of destruction in our private lives, our relationships, our health, everything. We may make wrong choices which give him a foothold, an inhabitable place, in our lives, but that does not mean that our choices are the only factors in the chaos which we sometimes confront. They are not. While we should always take responsibility for poor decisions and catastrophic errors of judgment, we should also realise that we are in a wrestling match with 'the adversary of God' (the literal meaning of *satan* in Hebrew, in other words 'Satan'). We should be aware of his strategies and be proactively engaged in thwarting them (2 Corinthians 2:11).

So then, exercise discernment. As you draw closer and closer to the Light (i.e., Jesus), you'll become more and more skilled at recognizing darkness. Whether your enemy is the world, the flesh or the devil (or a combination of them), fight—and fight to win.

It's Time to Wage War

Please understand that just because you are a Christian this does not exempt you from attack. Becoming a Christian does not lead you away from the battle, to a life of R & R far from the front; it leads you to the heat of the battle.

Some believers naively believe that once they are in Christ it is impossible for the devil or his shadows to darken their doorsteps. But this is one of the devil's cleverest deceptions. In his book, *Bondage Breaker*, Neil T Anderson deals this lie a decisive and terminal blow. He writes, 'if Satan can't touch the church, why are we instructed to put on the armour of God, to resist the devil, to stand firm and to be alert? If we aren't susceptible to being wounded or trapped by Satan, why does Paul describe our relationship to the powers of darkness as a wrestling match? Those who deny the enemy's potential for destruction are the most vulnerable to it'.

In 1940 Winston Churchill stood up in Parliament to deliver a speech to a house packed to the rafters. Hitler had risen in power and was making dangerous advances in Europe, occupying entire nations. Churchill needed to assert his leadership in an uncompromising way if he was to lead the country against the darkness that was heading towards British shores. This led him to write and deliver what is arguably his greatest wartime speech to Parliament:

'I would say to the House, as I said to those who've joined this government: 'I have nothing to offer but blood, toil, tears and sweat'.

We have before us an ordeal of the most grievous kind. We have before us many, many long months of struggle and of suffering. You ask, what is our policy? I will say: It is to wage war, by sea, land and air, with all our might and with all the strength that God can give us; to wage war against a monstrous tyranny, never surpassed in the dark and lamentable catalogue of human crime. That is our policy.

You ask, what is our aim? I can answer in one word: Victory. Victory at all costs, victory in spite of all terror, victory, however long and hard the road may be; for without victory, there is no survival. Let that be realised; no survival for the British Empire, no survival for all that the British Empire has stood for, no survival for the urge and impulse of the ages, that mankind will move forward towards its goal.

But I take up my task with buoyancy and hope. I feel sure that our cause will not be suffered to fail among men. At this time I feel entitled to claim the aid of all, and I say, 'Come then, let us go forward together with our united strength'.'

The first time I read these words, the hairs on the back of my neck stood to attention. Historians have recorded that both the Prime Minister and the entire cabinet were so moved that they wept at the conclusion of this address. It was a dark time indeed. However, the light would triumph.

Though Hitler is dead, the anti-Christian spirit behind him is very much alive and active. Evil still grows its roots in the soil of every life that gives it room to grow. It does not discriminate. We are all targets in the battle. The spiritual war that we perhaps unknowingly signed for when we became Christians rages on. And dark though the days are, we are heading towards a final victory. We must take up arms and stand firm. We must 'never surrender', to quote Churchill.

We have tremendous allies in the form of the Triune God, his angels and of course our fellow Christians. We have supernatural weapons of warfare in our fight against evil. We have God's empowering grace to help us conquer.

Above all, we have the power of God at our disposal, which the Apostle Paul says is the same death-defeating strength that raised Jesus from the dead.

As I close this chapter, please remember that we fight in the battle but we do not fight alone. Victory is the combination of our choices and God's great power. It is the result of human free will and divine grace in perfect unity.

So draw on God's awesome power.

Remember and be encouraged by Paul's words:

The Spirit of God, who raised Jesus from the dead, lives in you. And just as God raised Christ Jesus from the dead, he will give life to your mortal bodies by this same Spirit living within you.

(Romans 8:11, NLT)

Any thoughts on this chapter? Participate in the conversation on twitter: @pfsbook #wrestlingdemons or www.facebook.com/pfsbook

Chapter 15

BACK, SACK AND CRACK

Metro-sexual men in our generation make some extreme sacrifices in the interests of 'looking good'. I would certainly not count myself among the metro-sexual fraternity. 'Back, sack and crack' is a not a hair removal procedure that I would ever think of enduring. For the uninitiated among you, this waxing treatment focuses on three areas that for many men become too hairy and hence require attention. I'll leave it to your imagination to guess what these might be.

Unwanted body hair can grow in unfortunate places. For many years I was the victim of 'unsightly hair' myself. I had a few hairs on my eyebrows and up my nostrils that had a mind of their own. Left to their own devices some of these would grow three-and-a-half inches longer than any other hair surrounding them—not a good look. These unruly follicles needed to be dealt with. In recent years I have come to realise that tweezers are the hairy man's friend.

Okay, enough about that. My reason for using the rather uncomfortable analogy of 'back, sack and crack' is simple. The subject of freedom from unclean spirits in and of itself is seen as a weird and, on some level, a taboo topic. In many churches, people refrain from discussing freedom from demons. It is a subject better left unaddressed. It's weird. It's not 'seeker sensitive'. We treat it as if it was a metro-sexual hair-removal routine—something better kept out of the public domain.

Hearing about 'back, sack and crack' procedures—with all its talk of wax and tweezers—makes us cringe. But does this mean that we always steer clear of awkward topics, especially those that have to do with removing unpleasant things that have attached themselves to our lives? Maybe it's time to get over our reserve and deal with our demons.

Razors and Lasers

When it came to my unwanted hairs, I had to deal with them. I had to take measures to remove them, however embarrassing. The same was true for the unclean spirits that had attached themselves to my soul as a result of habitual sexual sin. With God's help, I had to take action against them. However embarrassing the subject of demons, I had to overcome my cultural sensitivities and go to the very root of my problem. The same intentionality I'd shown with my body I now needed to demonstrate in relation to my soul and my spirit.

Put another way, I had to move from dealing with the surface issue—sinful behaviour—and move to the root issue, which was the oppression of my soul by shadows. The Latin word for 'root' is 'radix.' It is the word from which we get 'radical.' I had to get radical with the sinful behaviour patterns in my life. I had to get to the roots of my addictions and remove them. In all of this it has been extremely important to maintain a sense of balance. I didn't want to attribute everything to shadows, nor did I want to go to the opposite extreme and say that nothing was influenced by them. As is so often the case, the truth lay somewhere in the middle.

Given that the root of a sexually addictive lifestyle is demonic in nature there is no way that we can find true liberty without the freedom ministry of Jesus. If we simply deal with this as a sin issue—as a matter of wrong choices—the upside is that we take proper responsibility for our behaviour but the downside is that we may never become fully free. It is like shaving unwanted hair instead of the more ruthless approach of laser surgery! The truth is we need to apply the laser as well as the razor.

True and Lasting Freedom

Jesus said, 'if the Son sets you free, you will be free indeed' (John 8:36).

Every person on the receiving end of Jesus' freedom ministry two thousand years ago would have told you that it was both vital and fruitful. Whether it was Mary Magdalene, the Gadarene demoniac, or the woman bent over double and bound by a 'spirit of infirmity', all would have given a rousing testimony about their true and lasting freedom. The same is true for me. I can tell you that the freedom from depression I now enjoy could not have been produced by medication or counselling. My freedom is compelling evidence of the importance and power of this kind of ministry, especially in relation to our sexual healing. I appreciate that many people struggle with the idea of freedom from demons, sometimes referred to as 'deliverance'. I don't really care what we call it, but let's not pretend that unclean spirits are never involved in our addictions, or that we never need deliverance to be completely free.

You may be comfortable with temporary relief from your sexual problem—happy to see your issue peak and trough like waves breaking on the coastline. As for me, I believe that he whom the Son sets free is free indeed. I believe that through prayer we can move to the place of complete freedom.

When Jesus and his disciples were ministering, they did not require people to book appointments. There was no leather chair that Jesus sat on as his patients received psychological attention or pastoral care, lying on a Roman couch. There were no long and intense preliminary conversations either. Bound and broken people came to Jesus, and they needed only one encounter. They were instantly set free.

I believe that we need to have more faith for such encounters today. While I grant that freedom is something we experience more and more over the course of our lifetime, I also want to say that there are moments when Jesus desires to give us a sudden and supernatural release from oppression. In other words, while the Christian life is a long process of transformation, I contend that there are crisis moments when God's power is suddenly manifested and we experience the dramatic breaking of bondages. So while I do not want to minimise the importance of gradual breakthroughs through emotional and inner healing, I also want to make a plea for us to be open to Jesus doing today what he did in his ministry two thousand years ago. In other words, let's be ready for him miraculously to deliver us from unclean spirits, especially those that have been playing havoc with our sexuality.

How then can we position ourselves for such an encounter?

Back, Sack and Crack explained

Back

Definition: the rear part of the human body

When we decide wholeheartedly to follow Jesus and focus on him, we turn our backs on our old way of life. We walk away from the rebellious and self-indulgent life of sin. Our focus is now Jesus, not sin. This again is radical. It means that we are not supposed to allow temporary resurrections of the sinful things that we should have buried. We are not supposed to serve two masters—Jesus and sexual sin. We must turn our backs on sexual sin and every other idol that we worshipped in our former way of life. We must put these things to death with finality and leave them buried in the ground.

In the 'back' part of the 'back, sack and crack' procedure, wax is applied to the back where unwanted hair has grown.

Strips with hot wax are applied to the unsightly areas and then ripped away. This is drastic and it is painful!

When we put Christ at the centre of our lives, it is not enough just to sing songs about Jesus being the centre. We must show that he is now Lord of our hearts by being as ruthless with our sins as we are with unwanted hair.

As King David put it, 'turn your back on evil, work for the good and don't quit' (Psalm 37:27 the Message).

Sack

Definition (literal): a large bag of strong, coarsely woven material, as for grain, potatoes or coal.

In colloquial English, the word sack also means to dismiss or discharge, as from a job.

There comes a time for all of us when it is necessary to have an Alan Sugar moment. Some of us for too long have allowed voices in the boardroom of our lives that have been destructive and rebellious. We have even supported these noises, bowing under the weight of their emotional and physical pressures. The truth is we have tolerated that habit or emotion to remain for too long. We cannot sidestep it and we cannot ignore it. Confrontation needs to happen and we must have that showdown moment when we say to that addictive lifestyle choice, 'you're fired!' From that moment on it must never be allowed back in the decision-making area of our lives. Even if that habit seeks to reapply for a position of influence, we are called to continue to make a stand. 'You've been fired and you're staying fired. Fact!'

When it comes to our sinful sexual behaviours, laser treatment is needed not just waxing. If we don't deal ruthlessly with our sexual sins and the unclean spirits behind them, then they can and very possibly will return. It is vital therefore to fire these shadows and their associated addictions and to do that with finality. As the apostle Paul wrote in Colossians 3:5, 'put to death, therefore, whatever belongs to your earthly nature: sexual immorality, impurity, lust, evil desires and greed, which is idolatry.' Notice that Paul doesn't say, 'put it to bed.' He says, 'put it to death.' Give it the sack. Fire these things permanently.

Crack

Definition: to break without complete separation of parts.

'That is why your sin will be like a high wall with a bulging crack, ready to fall. All of a sudden it will fall.'

(Isaiah 30:13, GWT)

The Bible tells us that sin separates. It sets up a wall between us and God, making intimacy with him impossible. If we allow sin to enter our lives, we must destroy it completely. We must bring down the wall between us and our loving, heavenly Father.

Like the wall in Isaiah 30:13, our sin can be almost demolished yet still remain in place. The wall is on the verge of total destruction. But it still remains.

When it comes to sexual addictions, what you don't want to do is settle for cracks in the wall. No, you need a complete demolition not a partial fracture.

Half measures will not do.

Nor will it do to go 95% of the way and then stop.

To use the waxing analogy, that's like pulling the strip 95% of the way off, but at the crucial moment losing your grip. In order to remove the unwanted hair completely, you are going to need to muster the courage to pull off that last few centimetres.

If you're equally decisive with spiritual issues, you'll destroy your unclean habits and you'll dispel the shadows behind them. The wall that obscured your view of Jesus will come down. As Isaiah puts it, 'all of a sudden it will fall'.

Let's Get Radical

I believe that we are far more tolerant of sin and shadows than our ancestors in the early church ever were. Today people become Christians simply by saying the sinner's prayer at the end of an evangelistic sermon. They make a commitment to Christ and then attend baptism classes. Amid great celebrations, they are then immersed in water as they publicly confess that they've died to their old way of life and been raised by God's Holy Spirit to a new life of following Jesus.

I don't want to sound cynical, but this is a far cry from what happened in the first five centuries or so of the Christian church. For the early followers of Jesus, becoming a Christian involved a far more rigorous process than this—one that involved repenting of every sin that had mastered you and every unclean spirit that had seized control of your life. This process could take up to a year. No one was allowed to be baptised in a public worship service until their lives had been scrutinised in this way. Only when Christ was truly Lord of every area of their lives were believers presented for baptism.

Let's just take a few examples to prove the point.

First, let's listen to a guy by the name of Crescens. He was a part of the council of Carthage tasked with determining the final Canon of Scripture (i.e. deciding which books were to be allowed in the Bible). He wrote that nobody was allowed to become a member of the church 'without first having been exorcised and baptised.'

Clearly baptism preparation classes looked a little different in those days. They involved every member receiving deliverance ministry—that is, freedom from every shadow that had been afflicting them.

Let's now consider Vincentius, another member of the Council of Carthage. He wrote, 'therefore, first of all by imposition of hands in exorcism, secondly by the regeneration of baptism, they may then come to the promise of Christ. Otherwise I think it ought not to be done.'

What's old Vincent saying here? He's advocating that no one can enter into the full promise of what it means to be a Christian unless they first receive prayer for freedom from unclean spirits and then secondly baptism in water.

Clearly the early church had different and more demanding expectations of what it entailed to become a true follower of Jesus. Apart from anything else, it meant the demolition of every demonic stronghold and the deliverance of every unclean spirit.

Does that sound a bit more ruthless and rigorous than what we're used to?

Let's now turn to a man called Hippolytus. He said this:

'When they are chosen who are to receive baptism, let their lives be examined... From the time at which they are set apart, place hands upon them daily so that they are exorcised. When the day approaches on which they are to be baptised, let the bishop exorcise each one of them, so that he will be certain whether each has been purified. If there are any who are not purified, they shall be set apart. They have not heard the Word in faith, for the foreign spirit remained with each of them'.

There you have it!

If you were in any doubt about the process required prior to baptism, you aren't any longer.

Our ancestors knew a thing or two.

They understood that a person couldn't and shouldn't be baptised until the devil and every demonic work had been completely renounced. This was not just a matter of words for them. It was a matter of power. It was not just a matter of reciting liturgy. It was a matter of receiving liberty. It involved dynamic, freedom ministry through the laying on of hands. Only then could candidates come to the waters to declare their allegiance to Christ and their rejection of Satan.

Isn't it time we became this radical again?

Any thoughts on this chapter? Participate in the conversation on twitter: @pfsbook #backsackandcrack or www.facebook.com/pfsbook

CHAPTER 16

SHIFT HAPPENS

When you look at your own addictive lifestyle, or that of a loved one, it's all too easy to become disillusioned about the possibility of 'shift happening'. It's hard to believe that anyone deeply entrenched in toxic attachments could ever become permanently free. When people say it's possible to have a lasting change of heart or behaviour, is it really?

Speaking for myself, I can honestly say that the very idea of experiencing such a seismic shift, such a radical liberation, was not even on my radar. I just didn't think it was possible. I had an eighteen-year track record of dependency on ungodly sexual fulfilment. I had spent years with waves of negative emotional torment rolling over me. Then everything changed. Suddenly I knew the joy of true freedom. A miracle happened which altered the course of my history. That's exciting.

In our despair we can easily look at an addicted person and think they're a write-off, beyond repair. But shift happens. Change, transformation, breakthrough, healing—it is all within God's reach. The Bible is choc-a-bloc with stories of people who were hopeless cases but who in a moment received freedom from an encounter with Jesus.

Take the Apostle Paul. The early church was familiar with Paul before he became an apostle. Even before becoming a Christian, Paul (who was known as Saul of Tarsus) was a

Jewish academic and revolutionary who vehemently opposed the gospel and those spreading its message. In the culture of the time, Paul would have been the least likely person to become a Christian. He was a Jewish zealot, and not exactly a candidate to be the author of a significant part of the New Testament.

For many members of the early church, the fact that this shift had happened to such a radical and infamous figure was hard to believe at first. They had seen Paul supporting those who stoned Stephen to death for his faith in Jesus. Saul, we are told, regularly breathed 'threats and murder against the disciples of the Lord' (Acts 9:1, ESV). It was hard to begin to imagine that such a violent enemy of Christianity could have turned to become its friend. Eventually they came to acknowledge that Paul had indeed experienced a life-changing encounter with Jesus. In the end they recognised that a phenomenal shift had happened in his life, from darkness to light.

Imagine that before Osama Bin Laden was killed he had aired a global broadcast affirming a 'change of heart'. He no longer wanted to oppose America; he now wanted to apply for US citizenship. Imagine Osama converting to Christianity and becoming a worldwide evangelist of Billy Graham proportions. The transformation of Paul from persecutor of the faith to preacher of the faith is about this improbable!

When the Turbo Kicks in

I'm not really into cars, but on several occasions I have been the passenger in a very fast car. Have you ever been in an extremely fast, turbo-charged car? If you have you may know from experience that a car's turbo does not really come into its own until a critical point. Your car may be moving at a certain speed. Then you 'feather' the accelerator and the turbo suddenly engages ... whoosh! The turbo kicks in and acceleration takes on a whole new meaning. Your back is pinned to the seat of the car. If you had stopped pushing the accelerator a moment earlier, the shift in speed would not have taken place. But you did and now you are flying!

Shifts can happen, and they can happen quickly.

One of the examples I would like to use to illustrate shift happening is the testimony of a well-known American preacher. Many of you will know his name, John Bevere. This is John's testimony, transcribed from his audio teaching series *Drawing Near*:

'When I got saved, God instantly took drinking, partying and profanity out of my life ... but there was one thing that he didn't take out of my life immediately. I was bound to a spirit of lust. And I was bound to pornography which led to frequent habitual masturbation.

In 1982 I married one of the most gorgeous girls that walks the face of this planet. And I think, 'okay, I'm going to be delivered from this now.' But no, it got worse! In 1983, I go into full-time ministry and it is getting worse! Now my job at that time was picking up guest speakers and one of the speakers that came to my church very frequently was named Lester Sumrall. If you don't know who I'm talking about, let me say that this man probably had the greatest deliverance ministry of any man in the 1900s.

Dr. Sumrall was alone in my van several times around the summer of 1984 and I opened up to him. I said, 'Dr. Sumrall, I am bound by a spirit of lust.' He then rebuked me with love. He did it like a father and I listened to every word he said. When he was done, I said, 'Dr. Sumrall, will you pray for me?' He said, 'Absolutely!' I came close to him and he laid his hand on my head and prayed a very, very strong prayer. Do you know what happened? Nothing. 'Well, I guess I'd better find a stronger evangelist!' No, you're not going to find anyone with a stronger anointing to deliver than that man.

That was the summer of 1984. Now, on May 3rd 1985, I go into a condominium. Someone I knew let me go there and

I spent four days in it, fasting and seeking God. On the fourth day, May 6 1985, I was delivered of that spirit of lust, and I'm free today. Thank God!

After walking in freedom for a couple of years, I started to have some questions. The most pressing question was this: 'Lord, I opened up to Dr. Sumrall in 1984. I bore my soul to him; I was not proud, I humbled myself to him and shared. Why didn't I get delivered when he prayed for me? Why wasn't it until I went on that fast almost a year later?' And the Lord started to show me my prayer life.

In 1982 I started to pray for an hour a day and there were very few days I missed. Then it went to an hour and a half and eventually to two hours. And my prayer every single day, for half the prayer time, would be, 'Lord, use me to cast out demons. Lord, use me to heal the sick. Lord, use me to win souls to Jesus. Father, send me to nations and let me win nations to Jesus.' And I prayed this way, passionately, for two years.

In the autumn of 1984, I hear the Holy Spirit speak to me. He interrupted my prayers one morning and he said to me, clearly, 'your prayers are off!' I said, 'I don't understand.' He said, 'son, you can heal the sick, you can cast out demons, you can win nations for me and end up in hell!' I thought, 'what?!' And he said, 'Judas left his job. Judas followed me. Judas cast out demons. Judas healed the sick. Judas preached repentance. Judas stayed when other disciples left. Judas is in hell. Do you remember when the twelve came back? The twelve came back (not the eleven) and said, 'demons are subject to us in your name.'

And I said to him, 'so what's the focus of the high call?'

He said, 'To know me intimately, John.'

So now my whole prayer life starts to change. My prayer is now, 'Lord, I want to know you the best a man can know you. I want to please you the best a man can please you. I want to know your heart. I want to love what you love. I want to know what you hate, and hate what you hate. I want your will to be manifested in me. I want to completely lose my will and just be a living vessel of you, to express your love and your glory to the earth.' And I began to pray like that.

I was praying like that for about nine months. So nine months later, when I went into that condominium, he said, 'your heart was breaking because you were hurting the heart of the one that you loved—me. I had become the object of your affection and love. Your heart was breaking in that fast because you were hurting my heart.' He said, 'that was godly sorrow, which produced the repentance that led to deliverance.'

What an inspiring and helpful testimony. John Bevere, a man known globally for his preaching ministry, experienced deliverance and came into complete freedom from the addictive pull of pornography and masturbation.

That should be compelling evidence that what happened to me on February 4 2010 is not a one-off case but an example of the freedom that is available to everyone who desires it—even pastors and leaders.

For John Bevere, shift happened. And it happened because he started to experience true repentance, which then turned into a deep longing for intimacy with God, the fruit of which was deliverance from his shadows.

If it happened to John Bevere, if it happened to me, it can happen to you.

The Tears that God Loves

John's testimony highlights something that we have not yet tackled—'godly sorrow'. The Apostle Paul writes about this genuine kind of sorrow:

*Godly sorrow brings repentance that leads to salvation
and leaves no regret, but worldly sorrow brings death.*

(2 Corinthians 7:10)

There are two types of sorrow Paul describes in this verse
in Corinthians: 'godly sorrow' and 'worldly sorrow'.

Let's discuss the worldly kind of sorrow first.

Worldly sorrow is what we feel when we are caught in
the act of sin, when our lies are uncovered, when our lack of
integrity is exposed. It is what happens to us when someone
who knows us well challenges us about an unacceptable
behaviour pattern. When this happens, our masks are torn
off and our true character is uncovered. When this kind of
exposure happens, we start to manifest the counterfeit version
of sorrow, worldly sorrow. This is not regret over what we've
done. It's regret that we've been caught.

You can probably relate to this kind of sorrow from your
childhood. Your mother told you not to eat any snacks before
dinner, only for her to walk in to the room to find you with
your hand in the biscuit tin. When you were confronted, you
were sorry, truly sorry—sorry that you had been discovered!
But that sorrow was not genuine sorrow.

When it comes to 'godly sorrow', the Apostle Peter provides
a great example. He made inflated and arrogant claims about
his conviction to stand by Jesus until the bitter end. However,
after he had done everything he could to distance himself
from Jesus during the arrest and trial of Jesus, Peter heard the
cockerel crow for a third time. He realised at that moment that
he had betrayed Jesus, just as Jesus had told him he would. The
Bible describes Peter's action after his betrayal of Christ: '*Peter
went out and wept bitterly*' (Luke 22:62, KJB).

The brokenness of genuine godly sorrow launches the
offender into a journey of restoration. This godly sorrow, in
its distilled form, is essentially a revelation to the sinner of the

way God sees their sin. We feel a sense of the pain that God feels. For the person who has been caught up in an ungodly lifestyle pattern, it is easy to become numb to the depth of our depravity. This was my experience. When God brought me into freedom, I was numb until I was confronted with the truth of how my behaviour had broken the heart of God.

Shifts rarely happen without godly sorrow.

God loves those who shed tears of genuine remorse.

The Shift Cycle

The teaching of Scripture and the testimony of people like John Bevere highlight what is needed if we are to be set free from our habitual sexual sins. There are no short cuts here. There are no easy roads. The truth is the path to freedom requires painful choices but if you are prepared to pay the price, God is a loving Father and he will give you the empowering grace to follow through on your decisions and to experience lasting freedom.

So what is needed for our freedom?

There are at least three stages which we need to embrace if shifts are to happen.

The first is godly sorrow.

You cannot go round this.

You have to go through it.

Genuine, godly, grief-struck hearts provide the fertile soil in which asphyxiating weeds are uprooted and the flowers of freedom can grow.

This godly sorrow is the first stage of true freedom. It is the deep hurt that comes to the human heart when it acknowledges that it has hurt God's heart deeply. I call it the 'devastation' phase.

Sorrow then leads to a second stage which is desperate and intense prayer for intimacy. This is the seeking stage of the journey. In this stage, the person who is sorrowful at breaking God's heart now seeks more of God's presence, more of God's love, more of God himself. Having recognised that his addictions have not satisfied his hunger for love, the repentant believer now fully understands that it is only the Father's love that will meet that need. And so he or she sets their heart on coming home, like the prodigal child, into the Father's arms.

This stage is what I call the 'desperation' phase. It involves much prayer in the secret place.

Only the Father sees this praying and knows about this seeking.

And what he sees, he rewards.

And the reward is the third stage, which is deliverance. Here God's mighty power breaks our chains and releases us from our slavery to sexual sin. This is a miraculous moment. It is the strength of God's presence on display. It is an invasion of the kingdom of heaven in our midst. It is true freedom!

Why does deliverance happen at the end of the desperation phase?

The answer is simple.

When we earnestly seek more of God's Holy Spirit, then unholy spirits can no longer stay in our lives.

Something has to yield.

Someone has to give way.

When we seek more of God, he will manifest his presence and when he does, every unclean spirit will have to flee from us.

The darkness cannot stand the light.

The devil is terrified of the Living God.

When we seek God's face with honest desperation, he will come and when he comes, the demons must go.

So how does deliverance happen?

This deliverance phase can come in different ways. In my own testimony you can see how my freedom came in at least two different ways.

First of all it came without any other human being present. I was on my own in my bedroom and God's power invaded my life. After many convulsions, I was delivered.

But then I received more freedom when my father prayed for me with the laying on of hands. When that happened I was set free from toxic emotions that had been robbing me of my peace for many years.

So let's not limit God.

He wants to deliver us.

How he delivers us is up to him.

If we position ourselves with devastation (godly sorrow over our secret sins), and desperation (seeking his intimate presence in the secret place), then he will set us free.

Shift happens.

It happens when we embrace the shift cycle.

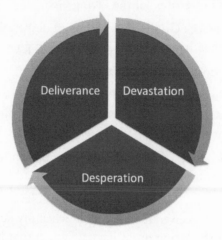

I wonder where you are on this cycle today.

Any thoughts on this chapter? Participate
in the conversation on 🐦 twitter:
@pfsbook #theshiftcycle or
📘 www.facebook.com/pfsbook

CHAPTER 17

INTIMACY ADDICTION

Following my discharge from hospital, I realized I had developed an unfortunate habit—an addiction to opiates. While in hospital, I had been taking a regular cocktail of morphine and Tramadol for weeks, along with other non-opiate analgesics. When I left hospital, I was no longer in need of morphine, thankfully, but I continued taking Tramadol regularly. It didn't take me long to realize that I'd become dependent upon my medication. I was tied to my tablets. I could not even leave the house without the comforting knowledge that my two-tone, grey-green capsules were coming with me.

By mid-January 2010 I made the decision that I was going to come off these tablets 'cold turkey'. Little did I know that within twelve hours I would be going through a horrendous rehab experience. Having not had my legalized heroin for half a day, my body was screaming, 'Tramadol!' at me. I was violently sick, hugging the toilet, shaking and shivering like a junky.

I was so sick that night that I was carted to hospital in an ambulance, its blue lights flashing. Within forty-eight hours, thank God, I had come through the other side. My body finally realized it was not going to get any more opiates and stopped throwing a hissy-fit.

At that stage in my life, I already knew about addiction—in my case to ungodly sexual intimacy. This had unfortunately been cultivated between my partner and me at the time. I had become habituated to a sexual connection and this girl and I were passengers on a rickety vessel that had taken a dangerous journey into the eye of the storm. We were pulled by passion and love into a whirlpool of sin and strongholds.

It was only my deliverance that brought me to my senses.

Suddenly I now knew that my addiction to sexual intimacy had come at a great cost to my soul (my emotions, mind and will) and to my spirit (that part of me that connected with God).

I had been looking for love in all the wrong places and it had almost destroyed me.

In the end, I had to recognize that I needed divine love, not sexual love, if I was to live life in all its fullness (John 10:10).

Biblical Viagra

Karl Marx famously stated: 'Religion is the opiate of the masses'. Though he intended this as a criticism, it is actually half true. God's people are addicts. But they are not meant to be in love with false and toxic attachments. They are called to be addicted to the love of God. That is the healthiest attachment in the universe!

Addicts are habituated to the attachment of choice, whether that is alcohol, narcotics, sex, or a cocktail of mood altering substances and behaviours. Addicts need a fix, and they will do whatever they can to get that fix.

My life now is actually not dissimilar to my life as a sex addict. In many ways my mentality is the same. I still have a dependency issue. What is it? What am I addicted to now? It's quite simple, and I don't apologise for it. It's called the presence of God. I am like an addict. I need my next fix. Even now I write this, I'm reminded of my craving for the intimate presence of God.

I need to worship the Father in spirit and in truth. Like the Samaritan woman in John 4, I have discovered something better, healthier, stronger and safer than sex and relationships. I have discovered the Father's love. I have become habituated to the true and only worthy object of addictive fixation— God himself! Forget medication. Forget pornography. And unless God specifically leads you into it, forget romance and relationships. The dependency we were born to live with, and the greatest, most fulfilling thing we can ever experience, is an addiction to the presence of God.

Today I have a burning desire to open my Bible and read it. In Proverbs the Bible is described as God's medicine for us. Though the medicine we are familiar with generally comes in tablet or liquid form, Biblical truth is ingested differently. You won't get very far taking it intravenously! It starts to bring healing and freedom when its truths are declared. Spoken out loud and mixed with faith, the Bible is a radical and effective remedial tool. IT WORKS! It may take time before you really understand it, but when you see the results you won't be able to argue with them.

At this point I want to introduce a picture from the world of medicine. A common medical practice offering help to those men struggling with the potentially embarrassing condition of 'erectile dysfunction' is the prescription of a blue pill. Any one unfamiliar with email spam filters will have received one too many junk mail messages offering them great value deals for this particular medication. That blue pill is, for many married couples, the means by which they can still engage in 'coitus maximus'. They are reliant upon Viagra for intimacy. If the supply of tablets stops, then so does the intimacy.

Intimacy with God is something that we need regularly. We are all in the same position; we need to take our medication in order to maintain intimacy. We have been offered a prescription for intimacy, and that prescription is the Bible. The Word of God unread is like a prescription unredeemed. The paper in and of itself does nothing for us. It has to be read; it has to be spoken aloud; it has to be used.

If I was a married man, and I knew that the only way I could be intimate with my wife was by my taking my medication, I think it is fair to say I would remember to do so. Why then do we neglect to read our Bibles when we know that our relationship and intimacy with God will suffer?

There are no negative side effects to reading the word of God. They are all positive. The Bible enhances my intimacy. Using it increases my longevity. Without the Bible, I would not be capable of directing my energy into intimacy with God. With it, my life remains stable and stays embedded in him.

Effective Medicine

Many people have the idea that to believe the Bible is an effective, authoritative resource for contemporary life is farcical. These people are convinced that Christians are victims of one word with three syllables—'placebo'. But this is the furthest remove from the truth. Reading the Bible does not create a placebo effect. It produces real and lasting transformation. As believers, we therefore need to remember that God's medicine is highly effective and can be taken for our physical, emotional and spiritual healing. Along with the Holy Spirit, it is the greatest asset given by God to benefit mankind. It really does improve our health at every level and enhance our intimacy with God.

How do we reap the benefits of the Word of God?

My son, be attentive to my words; incline your ear to my sayings. Let them not escape from your sight; keep them within your heart. For they are life to those who find them, and healing to all their flesh. Keep your heart with all vigilance, for from it flow the springs of life.'

(Proverbs 4:20-23, ESV)

Notice the four things that King Solomon advises:

1. Give attention to my words.

2. Incline your ear to my saying.

3. Do not let them depart from your eyes.

4. Keep them within your heart.

Let's take a closer look at these.

1. Give total attention to the Bible. Don't multitask when reading the Bible. I'm all for reading the Bible on the toilet but if that is the only time you read the Word of God, you won't get the fullness of its benefits. You need to give it fully focused time. Let the Word of God seep into you; let it have its effect.

2. Inclining your ear means you're prepared to listen. You have an attitude of humility. You know who the teacher is and who the pupil is. You know you don't know it all. On the contrary, you need and want to learn. And importantly, you're prepared to learn. We must put ourselves in a place to listen. It's an impossible task to teach people who do not want to be taught. You will consciously position yourself—you will incline your ear—to do so.

3. Focus, focus, focus on the Word of God, not on the TV screen, magazine columns, philosophers or random advice. The Bible needs to be your primary source of counsel.

4. The purpose of all these things is to get God's Word into your heart, the centre of the human personality. When we get the Word into our hearts, we start to experience the change that the Holy Spirit wants to work in us.

Faith comes by hearing the Word of God and if you don't have faith at the moment, you don't have to continue without it. You can cultivate faith by feeding yourself with the Word of God. Read things that will help you. Watch things that will help you. Talk about things that will help you. Listen to things that will benefit you. Focus on the Word of God.

When we are faced with anxiety, temptation, opposition, etc., before we look anywhere else, let's learn to rely on our divine medication—the Word of God!

Defence against Depression

By treasuring his Word, by valuing it and living it out, we are given the medicine which brings a life of freedom within our reach. This is not advertising spin either. The Bible is not a hyped-up sales manifesto offering impossible promises about a medical product that disappoints. The Word of God genuinely works.

God's Word is medicine.

I can show you how it has been medicine for me.

For one thing, it has been my medicine for depression. God has promised me

... a garment of praise instead of a spirit of despair.
They will be called oaks of righteousness, a planting of
the LORD for the display of his splendour.

(Isaiah 61:3)

The Word of God gives the prescription for despair. It shows that praise is the best defence against depression.

Putting on the 'garment of praise' causes our despair to withdraw.

C.S. Lewis once described praise as 'inner health made audible.' What he meant was this. The person who reads what the Bible says about the Living God and then turns that into praise is someone whose heart is healthy. Far from being self-absorbed, they are fixated on God. Those who are obsessed with themselves look inwards. Those who are fascinated by God look upwards. Looking inwards causes your heart to become unhealthy. Looking upwards causes your heart to be filled with life. Praise really is the audible expression of a heart made healthy by the Biblical truth about God. Tablets will never give you the results that God can provide through his Word.

The Path to Purity

We cannot have wholeness and holiness without a daily intake of Biblical truth. As King David pondered,

> *How can a young person stay on the path of purity? By living according to your word. I seek you with all my heart; do not let me stray from your commands. I have hidden your word in my heart that I might not sin against you.*

> (Psalm 119:9-11)

How do we take the first steps on a journey into purity? The answer is found here. We begin by storing the Word of God in our hearts and by seeking him with all our hearts. We begin by looking at our standards in the light of God's standards. In the language of Alcoholics Anonymous, we conduct a ruthless 'moral inventory' of our lives in the light of God's truth. In the process we face reality, we don't flee from it. As the Apostle James put it:

> *Anyone who listens to the word but does not do what it says is like someone who looks at his face in*

*a mirror and, after looking at himself, goes away
and immediately forgets what he looks like. But
whoever looks intently into the perfect law that gives
freedom, and continues in it—not forgetting what they
have heard, but doing it—they will be blessed in what
they do.*

(James 1:23-25)

The Bible is God's mirror for mankind. As we look into Scripture, we see our reflection. We see our impurities, our imperfections and our blemishes. This means we can quickly be confronted by our mistakes and sin. That shouldn't mean that we stop reading this life-changing book. In its pages we are not just presented with a diagnosis of our disease but a prognosis for our cure. God's Word gives us the solution because it is 'the perfect law that gives freedom.' We are handed the prescription and invited to take it for our healing. This means that we must not read the Word and then have a temporary bout of amnesia immediately afterwards. We have taken a look in the mirror, and we must acknowledge that this is an accurate reflection of what we are really like. It may be ugly, but this is our current reality.

Back to the Bible

In his teaching series, 'God's medicine bottle', Derek Prince says that we can ascertain how much God means to us by looking at how much his Word means to us:

We don't obey God more than we obey his Word.

We don't love God more than we love his Word.

We don't have time for God more than we have for his Word.

Our love for Jesus is directly proportionate to our passion for and hunger for his Word.

Is it time to get back to the Bible?

I pray that in my own life this passion would increase and develop, releasing me into a fulfilled life of liberty in him.

I pray that for you too.

Any thoughts on this chapter? Participate in the conversation on twitter: @pfsbook #intimacyaddiction or www.facebook.com/pfsbook

CHAPTER 18

PRAYER IS BETTER THAN SEX

When I make the statement, 'Prayer is better than sex', some might say, 'If that's the case Dave, you're not doing it right!' I would say to those same people, 'you're the one not doing it right!'

If you were praying right, you would agree that there is nothing that can compare with the intimate presence of God. You would be craving it. Intimacy with Jesus would be on your mind all day—more than anything else. If you're praying right, you spend time thinking about the presence of God, not sex, porn or your own personal gratification.

Speaking as a man who has spent much of my life feeding off a steady flow of sexual thoughts, I can promise you that God's presence is better than every other source of intimacy.

For most of my life, I was statistically more likely to masturbate than spend quality time with God on any given day. I was meditating on sexual pleasure, but any excitement or expectation about being in God's presence was far down the list of my priorities. Eighteen years of my life were characterised by regular sexual fulfilment and comparatively irregular spiritual fulfilment. I could not envisage a time when habitual masturbation would be possible to resist. Now, three years into my journey of freedom, I find myself in a place that could not be more different. I have by God's grace been free from lust in all forms every single day since my deliverance. I've enjoyed personal intimacy with God that has given new meaning to spiritual devotion. This has been my reality. I have enjoyed God more than a newly married man would enjoy his bride and it has continued every single day since my point of breakthrough. I wouldn't go back to my former way of living for anything.

I don't wish to be crude or offend anyone, but I do want to be clear—the presence of God is better than an orgasm. I am quite serious. If until now your greatest experiential pleasure comes from a source other than the presence of Jesus Christ, I have some news for you, 'there's more.' By pushing into the presence of God, you will eventually reach a 'high' that is greater than anything you have yet experienced. It's different, but it's definitely better.

Don't get me wrong. In the right context, sex is amazing. In marriage, sex is one of God's greatest gifts to humanity, and it's not just for making babies. It's for physical pleasure. Sex unites a man and woman, strengthening the bond of love between them and bringing comfort in good times and bad. It can be a truly wonderful source of intimacy and unity.

But we should realise that prayer is better even than sex within marriage. Prayer brings us into the presence of God. This is earth's foretaste of an eternal pleasure. There's nothing like God's presence. In it we find fullness of joy and everlasting pleasures.

'David, are you suggesting that my prayer life can be more exhilarating than my sex life?'

Yes!

The Greater Good

Do not deprive each other except perhaps by mutual consent and for a time, so that you may devote

*yourselves to prayer. Then come together again so
that Satan will not tempt you because of your lack of
self-control.*

(1 Corinthians 7:5—TNIV)

Paul's advice to married couples is that there is sometimes
a season when, by shared decision, abstaining from sexual
intimacy is beneficial. This decision allows focus to go into
prayer. Though Paul's advice is that this should 'only be for
a time', this verse points to the fact that prayer is of greater
benefit than sex. Sex may bring you closer to your spouse, but
prayer brings you closer to your Saviour.

The Bible is clear about the priority of prayer. We should
'pray without ceasing'. There is never a time when prayer
should stop, but there can be a time when sex should stop.
This is only for a season, but it again displays the truth that
prayer is better than sex.

Did you know that prayer is supposed to be an exhilarating
experience? Being in the presence of God is actually meant
to feel good. I am not exaggerating. Spending time with the
Creator of the universe and experiencing his presence is an
overwhelming, elating experience.

How do you respond to this?

Some of you may think I am introducing the prayer
versus sex comparison purely in the interest of controversy.

Some may agree with me on some level but feel I am over
the top in my description.

Some may feel highly offended and totally disagree.

Others will completely resonate with what I'm saying.

I want to dangle a possibility in front of you.

What if the presence of God can literally be better than
sex?

Taste and See

What if it actually is this good, and you just haven't experienced the fullness of it yet?

Please don't just take my word for it.

Taste and see that the Lord is good;
blessed is the one who takes refuge in him.

(Psalm 34:8)

If you were describing your favourite restaurant to someone who had never tasted its food, no matter how glowing the review you gave, it would not actually do the restaurant justice. Unless the person was able to actually taste it, your description would be at best a description.

Consider sitting in the Royal Albert Hall, positioned in the acoustic sweet spot, listening to the London Philharmonic Orchestra as they performed the most emotive of Mozart's compositions. Now imagine trying to describe what you have just heard to someone who wasn't there. How adequately could you really describe that piece of music? It would not compare to a person hearing it and experiencing it for themselves.

If you have never tasted the food in my favourite restaurant, don't tell me what it tastes like. If you have never enjoyed the London Philharmonic at the Royal Albert Hall, don't tell me what it sounds like.

Similarly, if you have never experienced the presence of God in the way I'm describing, don't tell me it doesn't exist. Don't tell me it's not better than sex.

Only those who have tasted and seen can tell you.

I can describe how good the presence of God is all day, but if you don't seek it for yourself, you will never know firsthand what I'm talking about.

Don't be short changed. This is available for you too.

What no eye has seen, what no ear has heard, and
what no human mind has conceived the things God has
prepared for those who love him—these are the things
God has revealed to us by his Spirit. The Spirit searches
all things, even the deep things of God.

(1 Corinthians 2:9-10)

The apostle Paul is presenting a spine-tingling idea here. When trying to describe the presence of God, he says that there are no reference points or familiar landmarks. It cannot compare to anything we have ever seen. It's greater than anything we have ever heard. We cannot fathom it in our thinking or understand it with our natural mind. This presence goes beyond anything else we have ever experienced.

Yet even though all this is outside of our framework, Paul also says that these things have been 'revealed to us by his Spirit'. That means we can enjoy the presence of God right now, not just in heaven. The Holy Spirit brings the joys of our eternal future into our present, daily lives.

Have you experienced these things? Have these things been revealed to you? If they have not, you have not yet pushed into that place of spiritual communion through persistent prayer; but if you keep pressing in, if you keep seeking with all your heart, you will get there. You will arrive at the place where you experience what no eye has seen, no ear heard, no mind conceived—the awesome presence of God.

God's Manifest Presence

Are you still struggling to believe me? Do you feel I am taking things out of context? Do you think my experience is a sham or that I am misleading you? Keep reading.

Let's look at what Jesus said to his disciples.

Whoever has my commandments and keeps them, he it
is who loves me. And he who loves me will be loved by

*my Father, and I will love him and manifest myself to
him.*

(John 14:21, ESV)

I still remember the day I read this verse and 'got it.'
I suddenly realised that if I search for Jesus and push into
deeper relationship with him, if I submit to him and follow
him, he will love me and he will *'manifest himself'* to me.

When I read the words, 'I will ... manifest myself to him,'
this idea turned me on spiritually. I decided that I would seek
God and believe that he would progressively reveal himself to
me. I wasn't disappointed.

The reason I was so excited by the idea of Jesus manifesting
himself to me was that I understood from my own experience
what manifestation entailed. When I was delivered of a
demon on the 4th of February 2010, I experienced a direct
manifestation of a spiritual being. That manifestation was
of an evil, unclean being and was frightening. What we are
being promised in John 14.21 is both similar and different.
It is similar because a manifestation of a spiritual being is
promised. It is wholly different however because the being
who wants to manifest himself to us is not evil but good, not
terrifying but comforting. That spiritual being is Jesus.

When I read that Jesus promised to 'manifest' himself to
me, this got my attention. I have felt the presence of God in
my life many times, but not in a way that did this verse justice.
I can now acknowledge that, in its distilled and undiluted
form, the manifestation of God that I now experience is like
a 3D version of what I used to know. In more recent years, I
have decided that if I can experience the manifest presence of
God—his peace, his love, his presence manifested directly to
me—I want a piece of that. I will press in to union with God
in the knowledge that I can and will experience more of his
manifest presence—Jesus undiluted.

Conversing with your Father

As many people have recognised, prayer is a conversation with God. It's a dialogue not a monologue. We are not delivering some kind of Shakespearean speech when we pray, attempting to impress God with our eloquently constructed sentences. Our devotional life should not be a one-way conversation where we pour out a constant stream of our problems and then walk away. If that is your pattern, it's not prayer as God intended prayer to be. Prayer is meant to be a conversation.

In authentic prayer we speak to God and God speaks to us. He takes great interest in our lives and he wants us to talk to him about everything. This means that we give him the right to express his opinion about what we're going through. We need to find time *every day* to allow him to do this because sometimes God wants to bring up things that we didn't even intend to discuss. When we connect regularly with him, we hone our ability to listen to him in this way. In prayer we become attentive to God's voice. Our intimate communication with him is one of the great mysteries and joys of life and faith.

A. B. Simpson very eloquently describes it this way, 'there is no wonder more supernatural and divine in the life of a believer than the mystery and ministry of prayer ... the hand of the child touching the arm of the Father and moving the wheel of the universe.'

Romance and sex in a long-term relationship can lose its fire. When you have known and loved someone for a long time, the flames can die down and the sparks disappear. Just like sex, prayer can become a clinical exercise routinely carried out between man and God and numbed by familiarity. It can lose its excitement.

This is what happens when we stop praying 'from the heart.' Our prayers may find the perfect combination of noun and adjective. They may be pieced together eloquently and articulately. But they are no longer real. They are like a fake spiritual orgasm. It means nothing.

The Book of James says, 'draw near to God and he will draw near to you' (4:8, ESV). We are told that there is a step we can take which will result in our heavenly Father coming close to us in intimacy. We move first and then he responds. We position our satellite in the right direction and he will broadcast his divine signal to us. His presence will become manifest to us. It is our responsibility to turn towards his glorious, loving face and draw near to him.

Let's press in and experience a new level of intimacy with him every day in prayer.

If we do, we will soon discover that prayer releases us into a realm of intimacy that sex never could.

Any thoughts on this chapter? Participate in the conversation on ✲ twitter: @pfsbook #prayerbetterthansex or www.facebook.com/pfsbook

CHAPTER 19

A MISSIONARY'S POSITION

No, not that missionary position! When I talk about adopting 'a missionary's position', I mean agreeing with the position taken by a missionary I know.

An English missionary to Hong Kong, Jackie Pullinger-To has had a profound and life-changing influence on thousands around the world. I am among those people.

Her book *Chasing the Dragon* gives a detailed account of her early years as a missionary. A catalogue of miraculous breakthroughs in the lives of key triad or Chinese mafia gang leaders in Hong Kong's walled city came about as Jackie started to obey God in an area of her life.

This miraculous series of events did not happen overnight, but there was a key moment in her time line that led to the breakthrough. The turning point came after a conversation between her and a missionary couple who were also working in the city. During the conversation, Jackie was asked whether she was baptised in the Holy Spirit and if she prayed 'in tongues'. Her answer to both questions was 'yes'. Jackie had received this gift in the early stages of her ministry in Hong Kong. However, she acknowledged that she had not been using it. The couple responded by strongly rebuking Jackie. They told her that by not using it she was being very rude to God because she had not valued or used the gift she had been given.

Challenged by this rebuke, Jackie pressed into using this gift of tongues regularly. She started praying in tongues for fifteen minutes every day.

What's the worst that could happen?

The result was a veritable explosion in her ministry. Suddenly the same simple words that Jackie had previously been saying with little effect were now being spoken with life, power and authority. People all around her started to experience radical change through new life in Jesus. Jackie now ministered to prostitutes and drug addicts in a powerful way and these addicts came to know Jesus. They soon started to practise speaking in tongues themselves. These former addicts found that by using this gift they could come off heroin with no withdrawal symptoms and find freedom in Jesus.

Speaking in Tongues

I was tremendously challenged by Jackie's story and when reminded of it by my family during my sickness in late 2009, I followed Jackie's example and began to pray in tongues for fifteen minutes a day. I had actually received this gift at the age of eleven or twelve but I had not been using it regularly.

For those who are unsure of what this prayer language is all about, fear not. It may sound weird but the Bible supports the fact that for the Christian speaking in tongues is supposed to be the most natural thing in the world. Consider the following verses:

> *For anyone who speaks in a tongue does not speak to people but to God. Indeed, no one understands them; they utter mysteries by the Spirit.*
>
> (1 Corinthians 14:2)

> *All of them were filled with the Holy Spirit and began to speak in other tongues as the Spirit enabled them.*
>
> (Acts 2:4)

Clearly speaking in tongues was part of the normal Christian life for the first Christians.

Now, thanks to Jackie's book, it had become a normal part of my Christian life too.

Within a matter of weeks my obedience to this call to pray in tongues for just fifteen short minutes a day launched me into the freedom that I am now experiencing.

In her own situation, Jackie had understood that there was a correlation between her praying in tongues and the breakthroughs that were happening. I eventually realised this myself. My dedication to 'adopting a missionary's position' created the conditions for my deliverance. The 'rivers of living water' (John 4:10) that were being stirred up within me flushed out the enemy's shadow and displaced him. In the process I was liberated from an eighteen-year sexual addiction.

This is the truth I want to offer you:

Habitual prayer in tongues + Submission to God = Deliverance from addictions and emotional freedom.

There is a significant link between praying in tongues and freedom from bondage. If you make a commitment to praying in the Spirit and submitting your life to God, then you too will find freedom from whatever is tying you up. Whatever the specific problem you face, it can be overcome through practising the presence of God in this way. Are you living in complete freedom? If the answer is no, have you considered adopting the missionary's position?

The Gift is for Everyone

To be perfectly honest, at the beginning of my journey in prayer, adopting the missionary's position seemed to be a dull way to spend a quarter of an hour. There were days when I was bored out of my skull for the majority of the time. I saw no immediate benefit to it. But I had made a commitment to pray, so I persisted. To begin with it was like cod liver oil—it didn't taste great, but I'd been told that on some level it was doing me good. So I continued.

God knows what we need more than we do. The prayer I was praying in the Spirit was unlocking the things that God knew I needed. It is my belief that prayer in the Spirit greatly accelerated my deliverance. Though God is sovereign and may choose to use other methods to bring people into freedom, it was the daily practice of speaking in tongues which brought me to a point of breakthrough. By constantly using this gift, I was inviting life to displace death in my soul.

In Genesis 2:7, the Bible describes how the Holy Spirit breathed life into man at the moment of creation. Man became a 'living soul'; he had the breath of God within him. God breathes this same life into the believer who exercises the gift of the Holy Spirit, the gift of tongues.

So who is this for? Who needs to receive and exercise this gift? It can't be for everyone, right? Actually, Joel chapter 2 prophesies the arrival of the Spirit on all flesh. In Acts chapter 2, after the Holy Spirit has been poured out from heaven on the Day of Pentecost, Peter says that this gift is 'for all flesh' (quoting Joel). This gift is not just for selective people. It's not just for the pastors or leaders of the church. It's for you and me—all of God's children.

From late 2009 until the present day, the use of this gift has become an integral part of my life. I have found it to be the only thing that works when I get that empty feeling inside.

Doubt, discouragement, fear, depression cannot remain rooted or carry lasting potency when I continue praying in the Spirit. Such negative emotions are an internal cry from my spirit, a feeling of 'homesickness for God'. When these kinds of emotions rise to the surface, this is the indication that you need God's presence. But when we pray in the Spirit, we centre our spirits on God's Holy Spirit and in the process our soul sicknesses are healed.

Perhaps all of us have a different capacity when it comes to our spiritual 'fuel tank' as it were, but we need to keep an eye on the gauge. The fuel light flickers, reminding us that we need to be refilled. Sometimes it's not convenient to pray when we get the signal to do it. For example, there have been occasions in the workplace when my fuel light came on. I would need to be in God's presence, but it wasn't convenient. I was doing a job. At those moments I would sneak into the toilet for a spiritual pit stop (my colleagues at the time must have thought I had a very weak bladder). I would go to pray in tongues in a quiet place, even for a few minutes. This was enough. The tank would fill up again.

I need the presence of God and only that presence will satisfy the feeling of emptiness that arises. Frequently while watching TV that empty feeling surfaces and I can only resolve it by switching off my TV and pouring out my heart to God in prayer. This results in a wonderful release of the presence of God and an equally wonderful relief in his fullness of joy.

God is faithful. He gives us a way to speak to him that frees us from the limitations of human language. We can pour out our emotion to God through this language of prayer. It might seem weird. But this is God's way, and for whatever reason, it works. That is why Paul says, 'he who speaks in a tongue edifies himself' (1 Corinthians 14:4). Speaking in tongues fortifies the person using this gift.

The Greek word for 'edify' literally means to build and restore a structure. Edifying ourselves means that, where there has been damage to our own structure in an emotional or physical area, there can be restoration. We can be maintained and rebuilt to a place of strength by prayer. Once our structure has been repaired by edification, the presence of God can be fully housed and contained, enabling us to live out the purposes and plans of God. We become effective.

This process isn't a one off event. It needs to happen every day and should continue for the rest of our lives. It's like those who paint San Francisco's Golden Gate Bridge. They have to recommence the painting process as soon as they finish it and the work never ends. Our natural bias towards sin will constantly affect the stability of our walls. Being strengthened daily and consistently through prayer in the Spirit ensures that we remain established and strong. It is in his presence that true restoration can take place.

A Lifestyle of Prayer

I live perpetually praying in the Holy Spirit. I do it more than you all.

(1 Corinthians 14:18, my paraphrase)

This verse gives us an interesting insight into the devotional life of the apostle Paul. Talking about 'praying in the Spirit', he says, 'I do it more than you all'. Paul understood that this is the way to be strong and effective for God. The more we pray in the Spirit, the more of God's presence we experience. The more of God's presence we experience, the greater our freedom will be.

Since December 2009, this method of prayer has been a regular part of my daily life. Starting with the fifteen-minute strategy that I have already highlighted, my appetite for prayer has continued to grow and is now greater than it's ever been.

Now I need to be praying in the Spirit for more than fifteen minutes every day. I don't do it legalistically, but when I need to pray, I do it.

Praying in tongues is in the spiritual realm what exercise is in the natural. If we only visit the gym once every six weeks, there will be no benefit to our bodies. Our muscles will not grow or develop. The routine won't make us healthy. Exercise was not intended to be an occasional recreational activity, but rather a regular aspect of a healthy life. We start with something as rudimentary as fifteen minutes of basic exercise every day, and within a matter of weeks we start to notice a difference. This gives us an appetite for more trips to the gym. Obviously we do all of this in addition to maintaining a balanced diet!

Exercise means repeating the same movement over and over again. Nobody argues with the fact that these repeated movements may be monotonous, or that they may leave your body aching. But equally, nobody would argue that they have results. Trust me when I say that your prayer life, despite occasionally appearing mono-tonal, will have powerful results. I should add that it won't be boring.

You start praying in the spirit for fifteen minutes a day. Before you know it, it starts to affect you positively. Your spiritual body shape starts to change, your posture, your mental attitude. You're not the same person. Signs of breakthrough start to appear and eventually the belly that you thought you could never lose is gone! How did that happen?

In the same way, exercise the gift of tongues. You'll feel the benefit eventually, even if all you sense to begin with is the self-denial required to initiate a new discipline in your life. Ultimately there will be signs of breakthrough. It's only a matter of time.

So cultivate a lifestyle of speaking in tongues.

Just Ask

So where do I start?

I want to develop and nurture the exercise of the gift of tongues, but I haven't been given the gift yet.

What do I do?

Jesus said, 'if you then, though you are evil, know how to give good gifts to your children, how much more will your Father in heaven give the Holy Spirit to those who ask him!' (Luke 11:13).

If you ask him, your Father in heaven will give you the Holy Spirit in increasing measure. God gives very good gifts. His gift of baptism in the Holy Spirit is a very good gift indeed. It will change your life completely. When he does, he will give you other gifts, such as the gift of tongues. This kind of gift is not a muscle that exercises itself. We need to consciously and regularly use it. It's our responsibility to do that.

So why not ask the Father now?

If you don't feel you have the gift of the Holy Spirit in your life, come before your generous, loving Father and ask him. Open your hands and your heart to receive the power of his love. This love is his affection. When your heart's been captured by that, all other affections will be eclipsed. There is nothing like the love of God.

Then ask for the gift of speaking in tongues.

When you sense some words bubbling up in your heart, speak them out however strange they may be sound.

Learn your new love language.

It's the language of heaven.

It's the language of praise.

When you use this gift as you pray in the spirit, you position yourself for freedom in Christ.

Any thoughts on this chapter? Participate in the conversation on 🐦 twitter: @pfsbook #mishposish or 📘 www.facebook.com/pfsbook

CHAPTER 20

WHAT HAPPENS IN
THE BEDROOM

If I could get a glimpse into your bedroom, what would I see? (Please don't panic! I'm not perched precariously on the branch of a nearby tree with a pair of opera glasses!)

The truth is, unless we are contestants in the *Big Brother* house, what happens in our bedroom is not for public consumption. But what if it were on show? If our bedroom walls were made of glass, how would we measure up to life in a greenhouse? How much would this affect what we did in private? Would there be a difference?

Historically, my bedroom was the place where sexual sin happened. Be it porn watching, intimacy, or solo sex, it all happened in the confines of my bedroom. For the past three years, a different kind of intimacy has been occurring and I am keen to give you some more detail about what happens in my bedroom to encourage you.

In case you're in the dark, the kind of intimacy I'm referring to is intimacy with God. Intimacy is something we cultivate. It's like gardening. We spend time nurturing our relationship with Jesus. We visit our garden regularly. We give attention to pruning plants and watering them. We sow seeds, we uproot weeds, and we make our garden beautiful. The result is a fragrant space that's a hive of life.

The alternative is an ugly unkempt space, rarely visited, overgrown with weeds and infested with rodents. And let's not forget those conscientious fly tippers who see this garden as the perfect location to leave a disused, mouldy, stained mattress or a rusty supermarket trolley!

Finding and keeping intimacy involves work.

Intimacy with God

The first thing that 'happens in the bedroom' is intimacy.

Intimacy with God is the life source we need. We desperately need to nurture our garden of intimacy and enjoy the fruit that it brings. This is why Jesus encourages his followers to find a private room and to draw closer to their heavenly Father in that secret place:

> *When you pray, go into your [most] private room, and, closing the door, pray to your Father...'*

> (Matthew 6:6, AMP)

This is what happens in the bedroom. When I shut the door behind me and enter my room, I have one thing on my mind: the Father's presence. I seek him over and above anything else and as I do I become more and more united with him. As Paul puts it,

> *The two, it is written, shall become one flesh. But the person who is united to the Lord becomes one spirit with him*

> (1 Corinthians 6:16-17, AMP)

Paul makes an interesting comparison. Having spoken about sexual union within marriage ('the two become one flesh') he then goes on to say that 'the person who is united to the Lord becomes one spirit with him.' Wow! What an amazing contrast. United to God, spirit to spirit, I have entered my 'most private room' and become one with him. In an intimacy greater than that enjoyed by a married couple, I am entwined with God—a truly astounding connection.

Bible teacher and author, John Piper, describes this intimacy using a passage in Hosea 2:

'Hosea 2:14-23 is one of the tenderest and most beautiful love songs in the Bible. ... But the most daring statement of all is the last one in verse 20: 'And you shall know the Lord.' To see what this means recall the peculiar use of the word 'know' in the Bible. For example, Genesis 4:1, 'Adam knew Eve his wife and she conceived and bore Cain.' And Matthew 1:25, 'Joseph knew her [Mary] not until she had borne a son.'

In the context of a broken marriage, being renewed with the fresh vows of betrothal (as described in this passage in Hosea chapter 2), must not the words, 'and you shall know the Lord,' (v. 20) mean, you shall enjoy an intimacy like that of sexual intercourse?'

Though this language is a bit graphic, it is certainly Biblical. We can know God. This means that we connect to and become one with him. There is an exchange so close that we experience a personal and intimate transaction of deep and private emotions and feelings. I don't know about you, but I desire more of this!

In 1661, the Puritan, Francis Rous, preached a sermon on 'Mystical Marriage'. In that message, he described 'a chamber within us, and a bed of love in that chamber, wherein Christ meets and rests with the soul.' This was Rous talking about what happens in the bedroom.

In this psalm penned by David, we are given a picture of his heart and passion to know and connect with God:

'O God, you are my God, earnestly I seek you; my soul thirsts for you, my body longs for you, in a dry and weary land where there is no water.'

(Psalm 63:1)

In the Sermon on the Mount, Jesus lets us know that if we have an appetite or thirst for God like that of David in this psalm, we won't be disappointed. There is no anticlimax. Genuine thirst for God will always be satisfied. 'Blessed are those who hunger and thirst for righteousness, for they shall be satisfied' (Matthew 5:6, ESV).

Pillow talk

When two people are intimately involved in the bedroom, they engage in what is called 'pillow talk.' The couple have made love and now in the wake of that they start to speak intimately about their relationship and future. This is often where some of the most private things are expressed. Hopes and dreams are exchanged.

In our time in the bedroom, we can expect God to open up his heart for us. These quiet moments should be enjoyed. It is often in a whisper that he speaks. We should not neglect to linger in the presence of the one we love, to listen to his heart and express our own hearts to him.

The Old Testament character Jacob has something to teach us in this regard:

Jacob left Beersheba and went to Haran. He came to a certain place and camped for the night since the sun had set. He took one of the stones there, set it under his head and lay down to sleep. And he dreamed: A stairway was set on the ground and it reached all the way to the sky; angels of God were going up and going down on it. Then God was right before him, saying, "I am God, the God of Abraham your father and the God of Isaac. I'm giving the ground on which you are sleeping to you and to your descendants. Your descendants will be as the dust of the earth; they'll stretch from west to east and from north to south. All the families of the earth will bless themselves in you and your descendants. Yes. I'll stay with you, I'll protect you wherever you go, and I'll bring you back to this very ground. I'll stick with you until I've done everything I promised you."

Jacob woke up from his sleep. He said, "God is in this place—truly. And I didn't even know it!" He was terrified. He whispered in awe, "Incredible. Wonderful. Holy. This is God's House. This is the Gate of Heaven."

Jacob was up first thing in the morning. He took the stone he had used for his pillow and stood it up as a memorial pillar and poured oil over it. He christened the place Bethel (God's House). The name of the town had been Luz until then.

(Genesis 28:10-19, MSG)

Jacob set himself up to rest for the night. It was late and though he was under the stars, Jacob was nonetheless in a private place. This was his bedroom. The canopy of the heavens spectacularly lined the ceiling and the moon was his bedside lamp. In the isolation of that space, Jacob listened to the words of God. It was time for pillow talk. Actually, God spoke to Jacob about something very intimate indeed. God revealed some of his most personal secrets. Specific detail was given to Jacob about the amazing plan God had that would unfold through Jacob's descendants blessing the entire world. Unbeknown to Jacob, his cryptic vision of angels travelling up and down that heavenly staircase was a picture of God's ultimate plan for mankind. As he slept, God revealed this to Jacob in the bedroom.

Many years after Jacob had this vision, Philip would tell his friend Nathanael about Jesus, the son of Joseph from Nazareth. John records Nathanael going with Philip to visit Jesus after they had heard about him.

Then Nathanael exclaimed, "Rabbi, you are the Son of God—the King of Israel!"

*Jesus asked him, "Do you believe this just because I
told you I had seen you under the fig tree? You will see
greater things than this." Then he said, "I tell you the
truth, you will all see heaven open and the angels of
God going up and down on the Son of Man, the one
who is the stairway between heaven and earth."'*

(John 1:49-51, NLT)

Jesus' words to Nathanael could be summarised like this:
'Nathanael, this is the reality: I am Jacob's ladder. I'm the
fulfilment of Jacob's vision in the book of beginnings. I will
create a staircase from heaven to earth, a way for mankind to
have access to heaven.'

Pillow talk is not always easy. Jacob's pillow was made of
stone. It was a hard pillow. It was uncomfortable, but this did
not stop God communicating with Jacob. We can have many
uncomfortable components in our lives that make pillow talk
very difficult. But even when we find our heads leaning on a
pillow of stone, we can still have confidence that God desires to
speak to us, despite the challenges which he sometimes gives us.
He will whisper peace into our soul and awaken our hearts. In
the same way that God spoke clearly into Jacob's future, we can
expect God to speak deeply and distinctly into our situation
and future. This is what happens in the bedroom.

Worship

*Ascribe to the Lord the glory due his name; bring an
offering and come before him! Worship the Lord in the
splendour of holiness.*

(1 Chronicles 16:29)

To literally worship your partner in the bedroom (even
if they are spectacularly gorgeous) would be idolatry. But
many do. They pour glory and adoration onto their partner,
revering the person they love (or the person they are sleeping

with) almost as a deity. For this reason, I think it relevant to include 'worship' on my list of what happens in the bedroom.

Worship is a part of my daily routine, but it's not driven by habit or some kind of monotonous predictable practice, or even by the presence of an entry in my diary. No! I am compelled to worship. I have to do it.

The foundation of my time alone with God is my worship to him. My devotional life includes the use of Christian worship music. I have a playlist on my phone that I blast out at high volume through my speakers and I sing along with passion. I don't only sing worship songs to God on a Sunday morning when I go to church. I feel the need to do it every day.

Worship is something that God enjoys and I enjoy it too. Perhaps this is because worship is an exchange. I sing to God about the amazing things he has done and demonstrate my gratitude; he reciprocates by pouring out his love and causing his presence to surge in and through me, filling me up. If I am feeling down, I get uplifted. If I am feeling discouraged, I am filled with a divine sense of optimism, courage and strength. I am met with the fulfilment of my emotional needs as I worship God.

The good news is that God is not Simon Cowell! He does not judge the quality of our worship by whether or not we hit the right notes. We are not performing when we worship and sing to God and he cares very little about vocal styling and technique. When we worship we are actually giving a gift to him that only we can give. However, we should also understand that God does judge our worship but not—thank goodness—in the area of technical excellence. He looks at our heart and our motivations. He does make a judgment of the offering that we bring. He judges the condition of our hearts.

Some people may think, 'singing is not for me. I'm not into singing. Singing is not how I connect with God.' Unfortunately you are going to have to get used to it. The Bible reveals that singing will form a significant part of what happens in heaven. Let's get used to worship in the bedroom now.

Rest

What else happens in the bedroom? Rest happens. Remember what Jesus said about rest? 'Come to me, all you who labour and are heavy laden, and I will give you rest' (Matthew 11:28, KJ2000).

At the end of a busy day we go into our bedroom because we are tired and we need to rest. We need sleep and we are refreshed by it. Every day of our lives there is so much to do, and the pace and intensity of a relentless life is overwhelming. If we were to ignore our body's call for sleep and attempt to keep going without rest, we would become dangerously overtired. Our spirit needs rest and refreshment and the benefit of time in the bedroom is that we are recharged and rejuvenated in God's presence. Intimacy with God results in rest.

Augustine was a philosopher and theologian, one of the most important figures in the development of western Christianity. He caught a sense of the urgency of man's need to rest in God. He once said, 'God, you have made us for yourself, and our hearts are restless till they find their rest in you.'

Robert Murray McCheyne was born in Edinburgh on May 21, 1813. He was involved in an explosive revival in the city of Dundee. It was a time of spiritual awakening where even children were caught up with an intense and overwhelming passion and desire to push into prayer and intimacy with God. This resulted in the city being shaken and changed by the gospel of Jesus.

McCheyne talks about the rest that is enjoyed by those who are connected with God and who enjoy the tranquillity of time in the presence of God: 'a believer longs after God: to come into his presence, to feel his love, to feel near to him in secret, to feel in the crowd that he is nearer than all the creatures. Ah! Dear brethren, have you ever tasted this blessedness? There is greater rest and solace to be found in the presence of God for one hour, than in an eternity of the presence of man'.

Jesus clearly couldn't do without this. As we read in the Gospels, 'very early in the morning, while it was still dark, Jesus got up, left the house and went off to a solitary place, where he prayed' (Mark 1:35).

Rest with God is a personal experience; when we partake of it we do so alone. We choose to separate ourselves from what is happening in the commotion and flurry of life. We are alone with God in the bedroom. We find rest with him in this quiet place—away from the noise, away from the distractions, away from people. We find rest in solitude, and that rest comes from a personal intimate time of devotion to God.

We are rested.

We are rejuvenated.

We are stimulated.

We are changed!

This is what happens in the bedroom.

Any thoughts on this chapter? Participate in the conversation on 🐦 twitter: @pfsbook #whathappens or
📘 www.facebook.com/pfsbook

Endnotes

Nights to Remember
Peter Horrobin, from *"Healing Through Deliverance"*

Like a Virgin
Joseph Prince quote is echoed in numerous sermons and articles but the wording used has been paraphrased.

Exaggerating Eros
Chronological snobbery—Cited by C. S. Lewis in *"Surprised by Joy"*

The Slippery Slope
Ed Silvoso *"That None Should Perish"*

Explicit Worship
Peter Horrobin from *"Healing Through Deliverance"*
C.S Lewis from the *"Weight of Glory"*

Cheap Thrills at a High Price
No citations

Bondage But not What I had in Mind
No citations

Erogenous Zone
John Bunyan from *"The Holy War"*

Sex on the Brain
Martin Luther quote from *"Faith Alone"* - A Daily
Devotional
Dave Gilpin analogy borrowed from *"The Mind Map - How
to Change your World"*

The Mass Debate
Dietrich Bonhoeffer quote from *"The Cost of Discipleship"*

Groping in the Dark
No citations

Team Porn
No citations

Three in a Bed
Kenneth Hagin quote from mini book, *"The Three Fold
Nature of Man"*

Wrestling Personal Demons
C.S. Lewis quote from *"The Screwtape Letters"*
Neil T Anderson quote from *"The Bondage Breaker"*
Winston Churchill quote from speech his delivered in
Parliament on 13 May 1940 in the House of Commons
Winston Churchill quote from "Never Surrender" speech,
delivered 4 June 1940

Back, Sack and Crack
Lord Alan Sugar from "The Apprentice" BBC1
Crescens and Vincentius quotes both take from *"The Seventh
Council of Carthage Under Cyprian"*
Hippolytus quote taken from *"The Apostolic Tradition of
Hippolytus of Rome"*

Shift Happens
John Bevere story transcribed from *"Drawing near"* audio teaching series.

Intimacy Addiction
Karl Marx quote, published in 1844 in Marx's own journal *Deutsch-Französische Jahrbücher*
C. S Lewis quote from his book *"Reflection on the Psalms"*
Derek Prince quoted from his book *"God's Medicine Bottle"*

Prayer Better than Sex
A. B. Simpson quote, exact citation unknown.

A Missionary's Position
Jackie Pullinger-To *"Chasing the Dragon"*

What Happens in the Bedroom
John Piper, Bethlehem Baptist Church, December 26, 1982
Augustine of Hippo (354–430), in *"The Confessions"*

Recommended Reading

Clean: A Proven Plan for Men Committed to Sexual Integrity, Douglas Weiss, Ph.D

Real Marriage, Mark Driscoll

Wired for Intimacy: How Pornography Hijacks the Male Brain, William M. Struthers

Sex God: Exploring the Endless Questions Between Spirituality and Sexuality, Rob Bell

Sexual Healing, Gerald Coates & Nathan Ferreira

Every Man's Battle, Stephen Arterburn and Fred Stoeker

Battlefield of the Mind, Joyce Meyer

The Mind Map – How to Change Your World, Dave Gilpin

The Bondage Breaker, Neil T Anderson

Spirit Wars, Kriss Vallotton

They Shall Expel Demons, Derek Prince

Soul Ties: The Unseen Bond in Relationships, David Cross

Healing Through Deliverance, Peter Horrobin

Freedom in Christ: Workbook, by Neil T. Anderson and Steve Goss

The Screwtape Letters, CS Lewis

Chasing the Dragon, Jackie Pullinger-To

Drawing Near, John Bevere

Printed in Great Britain
by Amazon.co.uk, Ltd.,
Marston Gate.